# BirdTalk

# BirdTalk

## Conversations
*with*
## Birds

## Alan Powers

*with illustrations by*
## Susan Mohl Powers

Frog, Ltd.
Berkeley, California

Published by Frog Ltd.

Frog, Ltd. books are distributed by
North Atlantic Books
P.O. Box 12327
Berkeley, California 94712

Illustrations by Susan Mohl
Cover design by Paula Morrison
Book design by Jan Camp

Printed in the United States of America

---

---

Library of Congress Cataloging-in-Publication Data

Powers, Alan, 1944–
  Birdtalk : on interspecies communication / by Alan Powers.
    p. cm.
Includes bibliographical references (p.177).
  ISBN 1-58394-065-0 (pbk.)
  1. Birdsongs. 2. Birds—Vocalization. 3. Animal communication.
I. Title.
QL698.5 .P68 2002
598.159'4—dc21

                                                                    CIP
                                                              2002013286


          1 2 3 4 5 6 7 8 9 / 08 07 06 05 04 03

For Sherley and Leonard Unger

"We two alone will sing like birds i' th' cage."
—King Lear 5.3.9

Some reputable scientists, even today, are not wholly satisfied with the notion that the song of birds is strictly and solely a territorial claim. It's an important point. We've been on earth all these years and we still don't know for certain why birds sing. We need someone to unlock the code to this foreign language and give us a key; we need a new Rosetta Stone.

—Annie Dillard
*Pilgrim at Tinker Creek*

# Contents

# Foreword

*Richard C. Wheeler is a world-class kayaker. A former Navy SEAL, he was Curator of the USS Constitution Museum, and has been headmaster of a number of New England secondary schools. He made a much-praised film,*The Haunted Cry of a Long-Gone Bird, *using the extinction of The Great Auk as a metaphor for the collapse of New-foundland fisheries.*

*Time Magazine named him a "Hero of the Planet" in 1998. He lives in Marion, Massachusetts.*

*L*IKE A*L* P*OWERS*, I *AM A* "Bird Person." Both our lives have not only been touched by birds, but have over-lapped with birds. Al whistles to birds and communicates with them, and I have reha-bilitated birds for about sixty of my more than seventy years. If a bird needs a warm place and sustenance while recovering from a minor injury or ailment that doesn't call for a vet ... I am its harbor of refuge.

I have often walked with Alan when he talks to birds, on the roads and shore in Horseneck Bay not far from his home in Massachusetts. He hears a call, listens, then whistles, cocks his head, listens again. Soon there is what might be called a conversation, as

Al listens intently for the bird to answer, and judiciously enters his own bird-statement.

What is he saying? What are they saying? He hazards some guesses, in this chronicle of his life as a whistling bird communicant.

In the equine world there's "The Horse Whisperer." In the avian world we have Alan Powers, "The Bird Whistler." When Alan whistles "like" an Oriole, he is an Oriole ... but he is also aware of and questioning his own place in "their" world, and whether his presence is intrusive. He has thought about the sound not just as sound (and he is a musician, who plays the notes on his piano and labors to transcribe the riff, comparing it to classical themes he knows) but as communication. "What does the bird mean when it says that?" he asks, and sets out to find the answer.

Most ornithologists or binoculared "birders" love the songs of birds. There are many books and CDs on bird songs. Who has not felt a thrill at the first call in April of a bird not heard since October? But few of us have the skill as whistlers to answer back, to reproduce a birdcall almost perfectly, much less to sort out who's talking to who.

Powers has a dry humor when he writes about birds. He takes the perfection of his bird whistling seriously, but humor is his métier. His birdcalls inspire allusions and references from Shakespeare, Emily Dickinson, Frost, English and American literature, the Italian

Renaissance, popular culture, bird lore and natural history. He listens to birds and replies, in the city as well as the country—in England, Italy, Europe, and around home in New England.

*BirdTalk* is a close-up and exciting visit with a man of enormous erudition and humor, who finds the natural world splendid. Chapter drawings of each bird are contributed by Susan Mohl Powers, which will help you identify the bird whose call Powers has been describing. You will delight in Powers' thoughts and Sue's drawings, and then want to go out and try to whistle back to birds yourself.

When I take care of birds and nurse them back to health, I have been their nurse, yes, but also their jail-keeper. They have been stuck with me—the bond between us based on food and shelter. Alan knows how to knock, ever so gently, on their doors, and sometimes gets invited in. For that, I kind of envy him.

—Richard C. Wheeler
Marion, Massachusetts

Mourning Dove

# Basic Bird: A Prolog

*M*ASTERY OF A HALF-DOZEN SOUNDS and intervals enables the enthusiast to talk with birds. The large fish-eaters, Osprey and Bald Eagles, make a high sound like sucking in through your teeth, lips somewhat pursed. Wetting your whistle can help. Be careful how you use this powerful, though faint, high sound. The hallmark of a predator, it is not universally welcomed by smaller birds.

Still with your lips pursed, form the sound of a "T" by tonguing against palate or teeth. This sounds almost like tsk, tsk, but is more plosive or "explosive." It's the sound most birds make when warning—whether other birds or their own offspring.

Now we advance to whistling. Start with the minor third, usually descending, like the first two notes of our national anthem, "O-oh." Stop before the "say," which turns the whole into a major triad. Just the first two notes, "O-oh." Now whistle it. This is perhaps the commonest avian interval, shared by many varieties from the Titmouse to the Oriole to the White-throated Sparrow (or "Peabody Bird") which more often sings an ascending minor third. The White-Throat inhabits pine forests like those in Maine and Massachusetts.

Next to the minor third, both on the musical scale and on the scale of frequent birdsong, is the fourth or fifth. Descending, it's a common, strident call of the Mockingbird and Cardinal. Ascending, it's usual in Robin songs, especially between the first and second part of its burbling chatter. Most Robins sing fourths, but in certain areas (like Providence, Rhode Island) I've heard individual birds sing perfect fifths. The fifth is the interval in the national anthem between the first "O" and the "say." Omit the second note of the "O-[oh]." Now whistle "O- [-] say." That's a descending fifth. If you slur or glissando between the two notes, you have made a fair approximation of a Cardinal call—that is, if you've whistled high enough, in the Cardinal range, around F above the C above middle C on a piano. Even the familiar, bluesy, regretful song of the Mourning Dove flutes an ascending fourth, and then falls back to the half tone higher as a grace note.

Of the Eastern American birds, the tonal register of the Mourning Dove most resembles Native American alto flutes of the Southwest written an octave higher.

Oscine passerines make many other sounds. (This taxonomic term covers most songbirds, "oscine" because they were once used for divination, "passer-ine" for "perching.") Some of these you can find ways to imitate. Many I find entirely outside my capacity. Gulls I can imitate by swallowing or gulping. One Blue Jay call combines a similar gulpy effect with a flutelike sound. It's a common call-note, especially in the fall, but I find it beyond my skill so far.

A word about rhythm. Some birds seem to be drummers: Pileated Woodpeckers, Hairy Woodpeckers, and various game birds like the one we heard every evening on a college hike in March. We called it the Blue Ridge Thumper (it turned out to be a Ruffed Grouse). Like the Song Sparrow's, its rhythm could be represented only by complex math, but it was fairly easy to imitate when we heard it. For the rest, musical notation gives a fair analogy to many standard bird rhythms: say, the dotted quarter note followed by an eighth note, roughly *dah-di*. Many bird songs sound syncopated, as if they're ac-CENT-in the wrong syl-LA-ble — especially at the beginning of a birdcall. I have represented this effect in musical notation by starting many bird songs with an eighth-note rest.

Use caution when responding to birds. They do not possess the same instincts or impulses we inherit from our apelike forebears. For instance, keep your dis-tance — say, thirty feet — when imitating a bird song. For most birds, twenty or thirty feet is roughly equiv-alent to a yard among humans. Closer than that, and you are up-close-and-personal, within the bird's urge-to-flee space. Don't talk to a nearby bird unless you can disguise yourself as a 20 gram ball of feathers.

Also, be careful about rising versus falling glissandos. Under certain circumstances, the one may be an enticement, the other a shooing-away. One mid-March morning I heard a Titmouse making its usual challenge, a quick descending minor third. I responded with its other call, an ascending minor-third glissando one half-tone lower. It returned my call and flew away a bit, maybe ten feet. With each repetition it kept retreating, I think in a "come hither" manner. When I tried its original descending challenge call, it did not repeat it. Both calls asked me to appear and identify myself, but the descending suggested a territorial dispute.

I assert here that almost never are two birds' calls exactly the same, so this book concerns ear training, as well. They may sound alike at first, but the more developed your ear, the more individuality you will find.

Oriole

# The Year of the Oriole

*I* AM NO SAINT, BUT I DO TALK TO BIRDS. They respond, most of them, depending on time of day and time of year. I am not sure I should tell you what they tell me. It is privileged communication, "For ears only," as government security might put it. It is a secret, an open secret.

One thing I am at liberty to reveal. They want in to sports competition. Birds feel that we lesser great apes have for too long bathed in our own simian glory. We have celebrated our own species, one limited, after all, to treading the earth. I've met Hummingbirds who would win all the Olympic dash events—100 meter? 200 meter? No problem. As for high hurdles, the Hummers laugh at them. Not very high. And no hurdle at all.

Birds are not alone in their desire for cross-species competition. During high school summers, I practiced running dashes on my grandparents' dirt road, a 7 percent grade near Norway, Maine, and then in autumn out back on a suburban soccer field. The dirt road held just enough incline so that when I returned from vacation to run on the level, it was easy, like running downhill. But at home on the level I picked up some real competition, my neighbor's French Poodle, Tart. That little curly-haired fancy-prancer ran fifty yards in under five seconds. 'Course, Tart never ran the full 100 yards straight; he always ran toward the hash marks, then to the opposite sidelines, and then cut back. A great broken-field runner, Tart's football career was hampered because he could hold only a kid's tiny football. For Olympic competition, the Interspecific Olympic Committee will have to certify dogtrack equipment—a fake rabbit or real ball for canine entrants, a bucket of money (or perhaps a news camera) for sapiens.

And sugar-water for the Hummingbird entrants, since we are talking here of birds. As I write, it's 5 o'clock on a July morning. The birds have just begun. Robins—it has been rainy, so they sing more—and distant chatterers: Sparrows, Titmice, Finches and Warblers, Catbirds and Mockingbirds, even Doves and Crows. Now join in the Carolina Wrens. They pipe variations on the "Mexican Hat Dance," the first part (or in classical harmony, the second inversion of the subdominant, IVth, major triad). Over and over. Sometimes they start on the last note of the "Mexican Hat Dance" triad. One day in late July I hear them do simply the first three notes of a major scale, rapid triplets. Over and over. At this time of year, the variations are freer. One sounds almost like a Cardinal, that glissando of a bird. There's the Cardinal, now. Today it's piping whiplike rising glissandos in rapid succession. The top note of the call lowers a quarter tone with each gliss. Oh, there's the rising staccato of a Robin on takeoff. Later in the year, "across the pond" in England I hear a Blackbird or continental "Merlo" make a similar flight song. It's in the same species *Turdus* as the American Robin.

As I said, I'm no saint, and now I must add, nor even a Cardinal. Then again, many of the saints weren't saintly. Not by Midwestern standards. Ever read Augustine's *Confessions?* Nowadays he might be jailed for failure to pay child support or have his wages—as professor of rhetoric, first in Rome, then in Milan—attached. Think of it, sending the mother of your child back to Africa because you're about to marry, and then taking up with a new mistress because the marriage is awhile off. Augustine was not as faithful as a goose, although some passerines would sympathize.

Now they have stopped, the birds. Why? The sun has not risen, though it's daylight now. A month ago they would still be singing this long after dawn. What are they up to? In spring they help the sun rise, they levitate it with song. It's their paean of praise. It affects the heavens. But now they have stopped.

# Assisi Species

THEY STOPPED. THAT'S WHAT THEY DID when St. Francis preached, according to the early accounts. Brother Leo, in the *Speculum* or *Mirror of Perfection,* reports two bird encounters in an otherwise busy, charitable, if anti-intellectual life. (St. Francis forbade books, even a breviary to "Friars of mine who are seduced by a desire for learning." [Habig 1198]) Near Bevagna, on his way from home-base at Porziuncola to Spoleto, Giovanni di Bernadone saw a field below the crenelated city walls, a meadow filled with birds—Crows, Rooks, Wood Pigeon and Orange-throated Bullfinches. As he approached, Giovanni/Francis did not spook them. They stayed. In Julien Green's account, not even a Magpie budged. Even when Francis started preaching to them, they did not leave. Of course they didn't understand Italian, though it is closer to birdsong than English. He congratulated them on their dress and spoke of how they should praise God for their existence. One had thought *they* could tell Francis how to do that. At any rate, the birds stayed until the saint dismissed them, so we are told. It is not too far-fetched to imagine his dismissal a sweeping gesture with his cloaksleeves.

What does this story suggest—besides the writer's anxiety about holding congregants' attention, a sensible anxiety because St. Francis insisted that his followers not study the art and technique of preaching? First, it tells something about time of year and time of day. Chronobiology. Birds flock together at various times, for various mysterious and not-so-mysterious reasons, such as migration. There is even a German word for pre-migration nocturnal flitting, *Zugunruhe*. If you were about to leave, like the Arctic Tern, on a 10,000-mile flight under your own steam, you might raid the icebox or flit about, too. Second, the account of St. Francis at Bevagna tells us about his manner and his dress. I have known one teacher comparable to St. Francis in this regard. He spent one summer tenting in Vermont's Bread Loaf Wilderness, his campsite part of the extensive realty claimed by a female moose. His Complete Shakespeare—almost pocket-sized, in eightpoint type—was wrapped in a plastic bag. Tall and darkly dressed, on the trail he blended in with the trees. His motions were circumspect. The moose had checked him out, as St. Francis's flocks had the saint. He was "OK."

I visited Assisi one January morning. Huge industrial cranes rose over the town, the aftermath of the earthquake a few years back. Many farms now double as hotels featuring agroturism. From a bridge over the Tiber—here, a forty-foot-wide stream—I could see Dabbler Ducks and a brilliant black and white goose.

Stopping in the lifting morning haze I saw small birds gleaning in the fields and flitting to small fruit trees. I talked with the great-great-great-great-great-great-great-great-great-great-great (this could go on for a page, since bird generation is so rapid) grandchicks of St. Francis's birds. And indeed, they did bespeak gratitude for the sunlight, the mild January weather, each other. Whether they learned it from the saint, I cannot say. If they did, one suspects they did not have the message quite right after all those years of oral transmission. (Recall the childhood game of "telephone.") All I said to them was a forceful, in-sucking *cheep cheep* like theirs. They seemed to be some form of Sparrow.

*Zugunruhe.* Back to my July birds' 5 A.M. silence. Do the many migrants among them, the Cardinals (in the Northeast), the Orioles, the Robins, the Hummingbirds wonder at the sluggard sun after their winters in Georgia or Florida or Venezuela? The most stunning silence from birdsong I witnessed, of course, during a solar eclipse. I cannot now recall whether it was a silence made loud by increased birdsong as the sky darkened. That would make sense, so it may not be true.

As for St. Francis, shall we say his birds treated him like an eclipse? Possibly, although probably more like a denizen, like the camping scholar on Bread Loaf Wilderness. With his simple clothing and reserved movements, and no hunting cap, St. Francis's *gestalt* or aspect was natural. Funny the difference a hat can make. On my morning walk I often stop to give some clover to two donkeys. I don't talk to them because a donkey's conversation is a spectacular mating eruption, a volcanic, sawing in-exhalation or *hee-haw* that denies meaning. His words are naught but the braying of asses, as the Bible says. So one morning I wore a new wide-brimmed sunhat. The donkeys would not approach. Who was this galactic visitor with the Saturn-ringed head they'd seen in their worst dreams?

## Careful What'cha Say

TAKE YOUR PALM AND TAP FOUR BEATS steadily on something in front of you—a table, a book, a Palm Pilot. This morning, early, I heard a call-note in that rhythm, three notes and a half-beat delay on the fourth, a descending minor third. *Deep, deep, deepuh dee.* (The *uh* is a musical rest, silent.) I don't know which bird it is, and I'm in bed at 5 A.M., unwilling to find out. Though I learn some dozen new songs a year—all for the same bird—there are thousands of songs I don't yet know. These occur in my own region, to say nothing about a province away. Like all language learning, I immerse myself in the unfamiliar until over the months and years it becomes familiar.

I have declared this the year of the Oriole. (Sounds like the desperate optimism of a baseball fan, but no.) Orioles make a plaintive call-note, a falling half-tone glissando. I believe they also make it on the wing, like Robins' staccato patter taking off. A few years back I pulled a St. Francis and tried to teach the birds. Recall that St. Francis of Assisi's peculiar gift was not listening to birds, but "preaching"—the word used in the early accounts—to them. Professionals easily credit this story. Anyone who preaches or even teaches can believe that the birds make as attentive listeners as most parishioners or college sophomores.

This Oriole year I gave up trying to teach them a famous symphonic riff. (Stay tuned.) I just listen, and if they are far enough away, I echo them. You must be careful if they're close. An echo at close distance chases them off. Probably half of all birdtalk, like people on cell phones, is locative. "I'm here; where are you?" Some birdcalls function as simple greetings, others as choral matins, telephones, even road signs and roadways, "flight paths," roadside route numbers, vegetable-stand signs. At the same time they can be elegant dress, ceremonial robes or stylish vehicles—performed to impress. Season dictates much. Spring call-notes roughly translate, "Get out of my tree!"

They just say it with much more style. "Yo! Flee the tree, see?" But on a cool fall morning, the Cardinal's quick-rising, whiplike call-note finds a distant answer. Is it his broodmate? His colleague? His son? Will one of them migrate, or did they both inherit non-migrating genes?

Back to the summer Oriole, who hits a plaintive call-note. He follows it with a cheery song, the rhythm of *Gaudeamus igitur* (the college Latin drinking song). The melody is a major triad starting on the second note. Inexplicably, the great nineteenth-century American "birdear"—pun intended—Simeon Cheney, in his enthusiasm, demurs about his song, calling the Oriole "hardly a songster."

> He is the most beautiful of our spring visitors, has a rich and powerful voice, the rarest skill in nest-building, and is among the happiest, most jubilant birds.... Hardly a songster, the oriole is rather a tuneful caller, a musical shouter. (Cheney 72)

Cheney does not appear to have read Thoreau's journal encounter with the "ones that Midas touched," nor to have heard the Warbler-like chatter I describe a page farther on.

# Symphonic Bird

I DON'T KNOW HOW HE DID IT, Giovanni di Bernadone (St. Francis, to you). He seems to have engaged them somehow, spoken *to* them. I tried this once—with Orioles, too. I noticed one who made three short notes and then two glisses a minor third lower. To hint at what I tried to teach him, the first three notes sounded like the first notes of Beethoven's most famous theme, starting his Fifth Symphony. The only hitch was the fourth note glissandoed down a half-step. And the Oriole's fifth note repeated that gliss exactly. I figured I could use the bird's tonal flexibility and whistle the fifth note a half-step plus a quarter tone *higher*. Bigawd, the bird did it! I had "preached"—what, music practicum, I suppose—to a bird. His four notes sounded almost exactly like the first four of Beethoven, except his glissando on the fourth, down from the minor third to the major. And, truth to tell, the fifth note was a quarter tone lower than Beethoven, but "close enough for union work," as musicians say. I repeated my "prompt," and he repeated his sluicy Beethoven. About three times. But having succeeded with the one note, of course I advanced to the descending fifth with which Ludwig concludes his phrase. And I heard ... I heard

... nothing. I tried it again. Nothing again. That last blew his mind, or it blew my cover as ersatz Oriole. At any rate, the Oriole could not conceive or perform such a note in such a sequence. It was uncanonical, *outré,* a gaffe, a breach, a solecism if not a *faux pas.* I may have sounded to him like an overbearing megalomaniac crazy to close the conversation, for after all, who was he talking to? Beethoven, not me. That eclipse of a composer.

I should add that the Oriole's instinct was very like the German composer's. That descending fifth interval comes much later in the symphony. Beethoven, like the Oriole, makes a long series of *dih-dih-dih dahs* in different keys before he gets to the descending fifth.

Perhaps less than one-fifth of all birdsong is imitable by humans. Although I write about that one-fifth, I do not forget the vast ranges of inimitable birdsong: almost all songs by Blackbirds, Warblers, Finches, scavenging shorebirds, Hawks and Kestrels, even Wrens. And hundreds of varieties besides. Even among the imitable birds, there are often inaccessible languages. Partly this is a matter of higher frequency than most humans— at least, than I—can whistle. For instance, Orioles have a whole other language they shift into after they have given their "dial tones," or series of them. Their second language sounds high-pitched, like a Warbler or Swallow or Redwinged Blackbird, though it lacks the overtones of the latter. This second, Oriole-to-Oriole "specielect" must be what Thoreau witnesses in his *Journals,* where he calls these birds "Golden Robins" (or because of their nests, "Hangbirds"). Thoreau records, "*May 8, 1852* Two golden robins; they chatter like blackbirds; the fire bursts forth on their backs when they lift their wings." (Allen 287)

It's difficult to know what birds are saying, though something can be gleaned by context. Admittedly, an observer's preoccupation colors interpretation. My friend, a father of nine, thought that the summer birds near my house were asking me to feed them; I agreed that they were discussing food indirectly, by staking their territorial claims. Emily Dickinson in one poem goes so far as to "hear" moral values from a Robin. The Mourning Dove gets its name from the mournful affect of its song for us humans, whereas it may be singing of pure joy, "like to the lark at break of day arising from sullen earth," as Shakespeare says in his Sonnet 38.

The first time I really held an extended back-and-forth bird conversation—echoic, granted—was with a very aggressive Titmouse. Probably because of the demands of specialized feeding and population density, Titmice are among the most aggressive local birds, so you can appear to "call" them simply by reiterating their call-note. It's a descending minor third, repeated usually three times. Return this call insistently and a Titmouse is sure to appear on the tree above you. When he does, you will know what you said, essentially, "Get out of my tree," exactly what *he* was saying.

Birdtalk tells us much about our own human speech. Our greetings, for instance, share something of birds' call-notes. The toney social party greeting, say, in F. Scott Fitzgerald's novels of the roaring twenties, "How d'yi do?" A greeting, yes, it is a welcome. But it's also a territorial warning. Whose turf are you one? The host's. What *is* the "territory" of a human call-note? It's a vast social network. Where are you in this network? If one considers the implications, an Introduction, in the old, static society, was a crisis. Best get out one's clearest whistle and pipe a repeated minor third, like the Titmouse.

As I write this on a July morning at the beach, I hear the *plop* of a fishing lure some three rods "down-sun." (We have the perfectly good "downwind," and for birds we also need solar-oriented adverbs.) Turning, I see a Tern rising. It fishes on calm waters by throwing itself like a lure. Can't see whether it hooked or taloned anything. Two Swallows skim the irregular wash or scree, small boulders that stretch a mile here. Three or four rods upsun, out past a pair of sapiens, a Cormorant surfaces, looking huge in the flat water, like a sea serpent on the borders of Renaissance ocean maps. Cormorants are the "Buzzards" for which this bay is named, Buzzards Bay. In flat water, the Swallows skim the water, too, for their favorite bugs. Mmm.

# Levitating the Sun

IT'S 5 A.M. AGAIN, A COUPLE OF DAYS LATER. I am home, listening to the first few bird songs of the day. Out front quite close—maybe in the shrubbery—a Cardinal starts its rising, whiplike whistle, like the first part of the old-fashioned "wolf-whistle." (You still occasionally hear this "*Avis sapiens*" *in situ* at a construction site.) Anyway, the first, rising part of the wolf-whistle—the *wheet* in the *wheet-whew!*—approximates this Cardinal call-note. This morning, I delight to hear him build first isolated whiplike *wheets*. Then two together. Then two together followed by a falling, Oriole-like plosive. Then two whiplike *wheets* followed by two plosives, or what I call "punctuation." If we could whistle punctuation, these would be exclamation points. Then two whip-like wheets and a succession of exclamation points— four. Next time, two. Then four—plus three. Like a jazz musician, he's building riffs. And he's also warming up like a jazz musician, or an after-dinner speaker. Meanwhile, the sky is ablaze with pink. He stops. He's done his job.

During this pause I should talk about gender and birds—the birds and the bees, if you will. I have used the masculine pronoun, and with a Cardinal it's easy enough to tell the bright-red, higher crested male, when you can see them. The whole point about birdsong is, however, that most of the time you can't see them. That's the fun, and the challenge. There's a brief period in spring before the trees have leafed fully, when, if you work at it, you can chase down many singing birds and see them. During this brief, leafless period I have found the specific trees or fields along my road where the Song Sparrow sings, and the White Throated Sparrow, the Catbird, various Warblers, and the Wood Thrush—though since I first identified a Thrush, in my teens, I have almost never seen one singing. They do it in the tops of tall trees at dusk or dawn or whenever it's hard to see them. Very like Robins in the rain.

But back to gender. It's a grammatical convention, and a choice. For several species with which I am familiar, a preponderance of male avians sing. Or chatter. Call it bravado. Even threats. For birds do live in a dangerous predatory world. Even the smallest—especially the smallest—participate. Their "participation," to excuse my euphemism, is often as breakfast-egg producer, or as food. Birds live in a hostile world. Anyway, I will use the male pronoun except where I have observed female birds singing.

A little after 5 A.M. again, and there's more chatter today—Warblers, it sounds like, busy and high, much out of range of imitation except by sucking in through one's teeth, crude and imprecise, but at higher frequencies than I can whistle in the usual manner. Maybe a Catbird, doubtless a Mockingbird, no Robin very close anyway. Their burbling, emphatic call— "hurried, few, express reports" as the poet Dickinson says—often dominates. As often they alone sing, or "play," because "singing" implies an expressive content that suggests joy. Even as I note their absence, I hear one, on the other side of the house, and some thirty minutes later. (No, it did not take thirty minutes to write this paragraph. I also put on the tea kettle and poured it.)

That in-sucking sound is like a sharp knife, to be avoided until you know its correct use. When I suck in one clear high note, it's as close as I can come to the Osprey and Hawk (and Eagle) call. Avoid it unless you want to send flocking birds—Starlings, Seagulls—scattering in caution or terror. If I in-suck a moist overtone, the sound approximates the most common of avian warnings made by all the passerines I am familiar with. One mild mid-February day I found the Titmouse on one side of my road following my mimicry along with its characteristic descending minor third. On the other side of the road, a Titmouse followed in the bushes without using its familiar call-note. Instead, as it retreated a couple of bushes, it scolded in the plosive variant of that in-sucking warning. Near it was another Titmouse. Had it already paired on February

16th? Apparently. Maybe the old British folklore that birds pair by St. Valentine's Day bears a flake of truth.

Now it's late morning, 11 A.M., and late July. Very humid air, 90 degrees Fahrenheit, while the ponds and creeks are nearly dry. I pass a Snowy Egret standing on the only rock in the local millpond, the only rock still surrounded by water. Maybe a foot deep. Two Egrets, three Canada Geese, a few Mallards grace the pond's edge. No Glossy Ibis with its long curved beak this year, though one was here the past few years. Hope he or she is okay. Talking to the birds makes one see their lives and their struggles. Each one over a year old does have an ideolect—each Robin, each Cardinal. Near the Ides of March I hear at an ATM a unique Cardinal in a bare tree; he whistles a rising triplet with a sixteenth rest between the first two slurred notes, C and D above middle C. Then he accents the fifth, the G. Of the hundred Cardinals I have heard, no other sang exactly that song. The ancient Romans might find it auspicious.

I just heard a sound, a short glissando from fairly high in my whistling range, too high for an Oriole. It could be the second part of a Robin's burbling call-notes. But no, he then follows it with five, then six notes. When I imitate these, he makes the distinct, longer (but still truncated) Cardinal gliss. Twice. Then he follows with the quintuplets, then sextuplets, descending a quarter, then another quarter tone. Is this an ideolect, specific to this particular bird, or specific to midsummer, late July? Or to this time of day, late morning, and this hot weather? I have conducted no double-blind study to eliminate variables, so I must leave it a question.

## Not Just Babel

ONE THING IS CLEAR. Many birds make some similar sounds mixed in their call-notes. Descending minor thirds are whistled by Titmice, Orioles, Robins, Chickadees, White-throated Sparrows (though usually those are ascending), Catbirds, and Mockingbirds, to name a few. But each has an entirely different timbre or sound quality. The Catbird's timbre is "thinner" than his cousin the Mockingbird's. Both the Titmouse and the Carolina Wren repeat insistently, obsessively. But the Wren varies his call-notes more, and they are triplets, often syncopated. Although Robins are repetitive in their way, their notes are impure and sidling, burbling, so they don't drive you mad in their iteration.

Contrast Titmice and Carolina Wrens, which might

be used like water-torture. (See C. Hartshorne on the monotony threshold in songbirds.) This only makes them easier to learn. Like calisthenics and exercise programs, or like piano scales, or like beginning language lessons, the songs of Titmice and Carolina Wrens instruct by repeated drill. "The rain in Spain falls mainly in the plain." *Ou se trouve la gare? Quanti anni ha?* "Thirty days hath September, / April June...." Repeated rhythm etches in memory: *Thirty days* and *April June* have exactly the same prosody, long-short-long or "amphimacer," the same as the first three notes of the Wood Thrush's pentatonic song. Start on the minor third, then the tonic, then the diminished seventh. If you play the black keys of a piano, try G-flat down to E-flat, then up to D-flat, which you hold for a couple beats. In the amphimacer rhythm, the first note should be elongated a bit too, *Dah-dih-daah*.

Roger Pasquier informs us that among the Bluebirds, Orioles, White-throated Sparrows, and Cardinals both sexes sing. Among such species as the Mockingbird where the sexes winter and sing in separate areas, once they again pair off on a common area, only the male sings. (Pasquier 113) As for Cardinals, I think I intruded on a domestic conversation in early April, after they had paired. One was perched twenty feet away in a leafless, red-budding maple level with my second floor bedroom. A male, he looked toward me—and the back of the house where they often nest.

He offered quiet mini-glissandos, which I returned. He uttered some more, which I answered with a Titmouse call. He took off. Possibly he mistook me for his mate out back, or stuck inside the house. Adept at dealing with the many mimics among birds, he wasted no time when he discovered the imposture.

Having observed Woodcocks at dusk in early spring in back of my house for twenty years, I don't understand Roger Pasquier's assessment of this species, "where the male has no role in nesting or raising of the young, the song and associated displays are only to attract a female for copulation." (Pasquier 113) The male certainly chooses an area where a ground nest may have the protection of thorny, creeping vines and other advantages. Perhaps the male Woodcock, with his spectacular display as of a ground army (a guttural squawk) and an air force (with seductive "kissing" sounds in his final "falling leaf" descent) acts only as a real estate agent, recommending a "good" (that is, prickly) neighborhood for the nest.

At any rate, Pasquier notes that, in general, "Little work has been done on whether the less frequently heard songs have meanings different from those the bird sings all day." (116) I endeavor to begin filling in this dearth. A corollary of this interest is why certain birds at certain times of year—for example, Chickadees in early March, on half-tone different notes—sing more than an hour before sunset. I have observed

Robins almost alone in singing in the rain—probably because of the increased availability of worms and the resultant joy. Do Chickadees welcome the oncoming darkness? Or is their competition for territory that for *nocturnal* territory—because their two-note song, differentiated by a half tone, sounds very competitive, like Titmice's interminable descending thirds earlier in the day.

After last night's thunderstorms, the late July birds are a bit late waking. I just heard an odd thing, an unusual creaky, croaky sound. Then a few quick, chattery sounds. Then the creaky sound, but more birdlike. Then several truncated whistles punctuated by occasional bursts of two or three notes in succession. It's starting to sound like a Mockingbird or Catbird. I think it's a Mockingbird waking up, warming up its voice. I have heard humans warming their voices on a college visit to Oberlin, one summer at Cornell, and, most lusciously, at the Naples National Library right next Teatro San Carlo. Through the large, open, second-story window-doors, and from across the small park you could hear the professionals rehearsing trumpet or voice for the evening's performance in another wing of the huge Palazzo Reale.

Back to tonight, coastal New England, late July. Last night's thunderstorms and today's pelting rains have filled the millpond where last evening only one rock remained surrounded by water. Along the coastal road, huge puddles. Redwinged Blackbirds mount the utility wires and stare either toward or away from the spectacular sunset—"sunset" we call it, one word suggesting unity, though tonight there are vast marches of differing cloud types, some of them hardly more than upward-trailing vapor, some cloudbanks that may run a thousand miles. The Redwings seem not to know which way to look. They're right: the sunset is a ball of orange fur. It's impossible to imitate Redwings, although sucking through your teeth makes part of it. Across the street in a bush sings a Song Sparrow, with its three-note initial call varied to two plus two sixteenth notes one half-step higher. Following this are incomprehensible, quick triplets, and so on. These sparrows have maculate, streaked chests—their central black spot worn like a heraldic crest or Olympic medal. Another Song Sparrow across the field uses the conventional, same three notes, followed by five-note bursts, first a half-step lower. Every year one sings from a couple of trees bordering two fields near my home. Two months ago the song of this homonymous sparrow had the rhythm of a Ping-Pong ball left to bounce on its own: roughly, duh ... duh-dih ... dih-di-di-di ... dididi-didi. It's the rhythm of a mathematical $e$-curve, an exponentially damped oscillation. The Song Sparrow. A Ping-Pong ball, but bright notes sometimes descending, perhaps by quarter tones.

# Mall Birds

LATE IN THE DAY, WELL AFTER 7 P.M., I drive to a local mall for a printer cartridge. As I open my car door, I hear a glissando call-note sounding high. It's also emanating from a height, a bird in the top of some dead branches of an otherwise fine tree. Outlined black against the pre-sunset, the bird switches its tail nervously. Not an Oriole. The tone seems much higher than an Oriole's, though later when I check it on my piano at home, it's perhaps only one tone higher, around a D above middle C. It's more piercing than an Oriole's. With my binoculars I can see it's a Redwinged Blackbird. And from the bushes I hear the unmistakable meow of a Catbird. Here I am in a mall parking lot and the familiar birds have nested nearby and found some food. What's that swamp-dwelling Redwing doing here? Maybe there's a swamp nearby, or maybe this mall used to be a swamp. More likely. Generations of this bird have returned here, even after most of the swamp was filled. I know the same species return to the exact same tree or grove or field along my road, year after year.

How long has this continued? The life of a specific tree sets that limit, a couple of hundred years at the very most. Two trees aged two centuries stand along this road, but most others are no older than a half-century. One of the ancient trees rises nearly a hundred feet, an oak. I do hear birds as I pass it, but no specific ones. What if the same species has returned to the same area for a millennium? Keats speculates as much, not about location, but about his nightingale's song: "The voice I hear this passing night was heard / In ancient days by emperor and clown.... " Perhaps even, he continues, the Biblical bird referred to in the book of *Ruth*.

The next morning after my mall visit, late (for birds) around 7:30. As I walk along my road I hear a syncopated, offbeat (not downbeat) descending minor third, the second and third note the same, and twice as fast as the first: *uhdee dih-dih* (again, the "uh" is a rest). Repeated. Then a fainter one up a half-step. This is it—dueling Chickadees. They continue, the one sticking to his tones, the other echoic, but in a different key. Together it's a canon. Lovely, too.

Having passed the consort of Chickadees, I hear out beyond two stone walls a call I haven't heard this year until now. Like the Chickadee battle-song, this one is syncopated, with a downbeat rest followed by an eighth note, down one full tone to a quarter note, both repeated once, ending on the fifth note, the same it began on.

This is a simple series. I didn't know what bird it was until after I mimicked it and it continued by glissan-doing those two notes and following with a Robin's burble.

One perfect day in late July, I hear a racket at the woodsy end of my house. The noise is a constant, fairly high-pitched *cheep*ing by more than one bird. When I reach the trees, I hear this *cheep*ing near the ground, in the bushes, and then suddenly overhead with some accompanying flitting. Looking up, I see a little bird coming closer, descending from higher in the tree over me. It lands on a branch maybe eight feet away, fans open its tail to draw attention. This is clearly an attempt to distract me from nestlings nearby. It's work-ing. But I do see another bird flitting behind it maybe a yard. It's making the same *cheep*ing, but it has streaks all down its breast—the young of the species, as clearly delineated as a prep school uniform. These are little Chipping Sparrows, with bright streaks over their eyes and forked tails, good for distracting . . . me. Here's a two-week-old creature—at most—following its parent who is doing its best to fend off the myriad threats. I am one, so I retreat back to my porch.

In August near the remnants of woods and a shack by a new mall twenty-five miles from New York City, I hear Crows and Goldfinches. I see a Mockingbird. They have adapted—or have they just not left yet? The diner has been open just a month. Today is muggy, thundershowers expected. The abundant thistle may cause celebratory flight songs from the Goldfinch. Surely Robins sing in the rain anticipating and celebrating the abundance of their vermiform repast. I can't remember hearing such a wealth of Goldfinch vocalization. But that is the way it is with birdsong. You are entirely unaware of it until you associate it with its specific singer. Once you do, you notice it all the time (unless it's a stranger just passin' through).

## Homo Homini Lupus

THE BIRD WORLD IS HARSH. If "man is the wolf of man," birds are surely the wolves of birds: *Avis avibus lupus*. I have seen a small bird destroy a nesting Robin's day, a bird no larger than the Robin itself, a small Hawk. A Sparrow Hawk or Kestrel came in no more than five feet in altitude, directly into a spruce tree Robin's nest, and left with one of its young. It happened fast. There was no air-raid warning or ambulance siren. Not even the usual bird warnings, the *cheep*ing and *keck*ing. The Robins were out foraging. Such a small threat, not my image of hostility at all. I'd expect trouble from a large circling Hawk, but a little one? Believe it.

Since that little encounter twenty feet from my back-door, I view every bird encounter differently. Now I know why you commonly see Purple Grackles or Starlings chasing Crows. Or Sparrows chasing a Blue Jay. Crows chasing Red-tailed Hawks. Any smaller bird chasing any larger. It's not a game. Professional tracker Jon Young explains most bird language, including flight patterns, in terms of survival. The major exceptions to this warfare of bird eating bird are fish-eaters such as Osprey and Bald Eagle. Shakespeare compares his most aggressive (and undemocratic) hero Coriolanus to the fish-hawk, "I think he'll be to Rome / As is the osprey to the fish, who takes it / By sovereignty of nature." *(Cor. 4.7.33)* (I'm sure the fish would chase them if they could.)

One afternoon in midsummer I hear the high in-sucking-between-teeth sound of an Osprey maybe a hundred yards over me. Straining to look up while avoiding the sun, I see what looks like a smaller bird chasing an Osprey. As I watch, the Osprey seems first to gain on its pursuer; then the pursuer seems to lose altitude fast. Now I realize it's something the Fish Hawk has dropped. Thump, it lands maybe thirty feet away, luckily just before the woods and bushes. Hurrying to the spot, I find the tail half of a fish, maybe six inches long, five wide. The Osprey's talons have ripped it in half. Possibly the fish struggled and the Osprey gripped harder. The upshot is an Osprey-style filet, jagged and raw-fleshed.

Early on the first day of August I hear a descending minor third, dih-dah-dah. I have not heard this for awhile, yet its timbre is the now familiar Carolina Wren's.

I wonder why it has altered its call. Perhaps because it was cool last night, in the 50s. Perhaps because of the time of year and the sun angle (it's just before dawn). An hour later when I walk down the road, I hear something on the wing over an open field by some camps. I get out my binoculars, but can pick out only a blur, grayish. When another lands in the top of a small nearby tree, I see to my surprise it's a Goldfinch. Birds on the wing so often look gray-and-white from below, even Goldfinches. Its inflight call sounds like four or five descending half tones or even quarter tones. The first and second of these seem syncopated, with the second accented. In other words, there seems to be a rest before the first note. Or consider a series of five notes, quintuplets, the first a rest.

Now at the beginning of August I hear the characteristic onomastic song of the Chickadee. Not primarily a spring song, we tend to hear *chik-a-dee-dee* in fall or winter, *pace* Barry MacKay who hears it year-round. (27) Still, he notes—no pun intended—that the breeding "song" of the Chickadee is the two long notes so familiar, so often confused with the Phoebe. (Mathews 219) Written an octave lower, they are:

I first recall these from perhaps third grade. I may have heard them in Maine, though, even earlier. Schuyler Mathews is eloquent on the beauty of these two notes.

> Poor tuneless Phoebe is intellectually incapable of such a perfectly musical bit as this. Mr. Cheney says of these two notes, "never were purer tones heard on earth." Indeed, few small birds whistle their songs as clearly, and separate the tones by such lucid intervals. (219)

He continues with praise of the Chickadee's musicianship, "he knows the value of a well-sustained half-note, another point which should be scored in the little musician's favor," in contrast to the Canary's "hemi-demi-semi-quavers every tone within the compass of an octave." (219) But the human response to this consummate Chickadee beauty varies. MacKay is not convinced, feeling the two notes "a sad, little two-note call that, to my ear, sounds *sooo-sadd.*" (28)

Usually very accurate, Mathews, in his *Field Book* makes occasional unwarranted cultural assumptions that interfere with his observations. For example, he states flat-out that "the Cowbird has no song; his nearest approach to music is a sort of guttural murmuring.... Why should he have either? The bird has no song—no mate to call. He is a polygamist, a bird of no principles, a 'low-down' character." (53) To the contrary, once in mid-April I heard a lovely call reversing the Goldfinch flight song by rising one tone, *deee-dihdih*. A minute later, having drawn me away from my porch and feeder, The Cowbird appeared at the top of a juniper with his grayer mate, who flew to my feeder, there devouring seeds. They were just back from migration, and they were hungry. Their talk was somewhat like a Starling's.

So tricky is interspecific communication. We project, say, the "mourning" on the perfectly contented call of the Mourning Dove. We bring our associations to the songs. For me, there is nothing more beautiful than the White-throated Sparrow's rising minor third and triplet. They take me back immediately to the rural Maine of my childhood, the piney woods. For others, they may speak of isolation and desolation. Similarly with the Wood Thrush. The first one I recall hearing was in the Berkshires, in Beckett, Massachusetts.

Birds are tied to the solar calendar as well as to climate; for example, the English Robin's so-called "spring song" begins in late December. This we learn in David Lack's *The Life of the Robin*:

> The spring song of the robin starts near the end of December and continues until about the middle of June. The autumn song, which is thinner and less rich, is first heard in late July from some of the young birds, the adult robins starting about a fortnight later. It is continued throughout the autumn, but is rather feeble in early winter, until the spring song suddenly starts again in late December. . . . The above dates refer to South Devon and are rather different in other parts of England. (34)

Now on a hazy day in early August I hear several "new" songs or adaptations of earlier ones. I can't say which of these are fall (winter) songs. I do hear a rising variation of the Song Sparrow, whereas in spring the one on my road, for years, has always descended with its increasingly rapid, damped Ping-Pong-ball rhythm after its three piping call-notes. Here's his rising variant:

I hear nearby another rising interval, starting on the same note, but "thinner." I see a Warbler. Back home, I hear "My Momma done tol' me."

I can tell from the timbre it's a Carolina Wren. When I imitate it, it makes a descending *shree* almost like a Blackbird. This I cannot imitate. I have never heard such from a Carolina Wren. Could it be, as Mr. Lack says, the young of the species anticipating a fall song, or even identifying its brood?

With all this birdtalk, might I be "the Man who Thought he Was a Bird"? This is an ancient medical case about which noted physicians and philosophers propounded cures. In his work *On Chronic Diseases* or *Tardae Passiones,* Caelius Aurelianus lists many types of *mania* or insanity (my translation):

> So some maniac thinks himself a sparrow, another a rooster in a henhouse, another a pot, another a brick, one a god, another a tragic or comic actor, even a blade of grass bearing the weight of the universe. . . .
>
> *Sic denique furens alius se passerem existimavit, alius gallum gallinaceum, alius fictile, alius laterem, alius deum, alius oratorem, alius tragoedum vel*

38

*comoedum, alius stipulam ferens mundi se centrum*
*[censum S sceptrum Haller] tenere.* (Caelius 540)

No, not a Sparrow. When I fly in my dreams, I am
rather cumbersome in flight, more like a Heron or
Cormorant with wet wings. Birds and flight appeal
to our irrational brethren, as well as our wisest (see
Chapter 6, "Avitherapy"). As for a rooster in a hen-
house, doesn't every adolescent male feel that?

The first week of school crossing the sunny parking lot I hear a piped, staccato descending major third.
Turning around, I see a Blue Jay at the top of a twenty-
five foot tree. I've heard just the first staccato note for
a week or two in early spring, but this seems to be the
fall variation. A week later as I leave campus after too
many classes, I hear the same call, and mention it to a
student who is standing nearby, her two children asleep
in the car. I imitate the call and remark, "That's a Blue
Jay." She's surprised, because it's not their usual jeer.
After I echo it three or four times, worried I might wake
the kids, the Jay swoops from a grove of scrub oak
some fifty yards away. It crosses in front of us some
forty feet away and maybe thirty feet up, and then it
lands on a tall lamppost. It has checked us out. What
did it conclude? I am no threat to its feeding territory?
I am not one of its brood? I am not a bona fide Jay?
Probably all of the above.

By early October, the remaining birds—Blue Jays,
Carolina Wrens, Chickadees, some Catbirds (those that

migrate may have genetically inherited a gene for migration!), some Sparrows (the White-throated, but not the Song)—offer their spare morning songs. But after a miserable northeaster, after a night in the 40s, the day opens with bright sunlight around 7 o'clock, and a bird scolds with its *tchk, tchk*—probably at a neighbor's cat. In the trees to our east that catch the first sunlight, a Carolina Wren offers its triplets. A Jay pipes its resonant, overtone-rich call. They appear to be greeting the sun; they appear to be cheered. Surely we would not presume too much to call this, in fact, *singing*.

A week later, rounding the bend amidst yellowing and rusting leaves, a haze of bright sun glows in the lifting fog over the rattling cornstalks. It's about 8 A.M., an hour after sunrise. Birds chatter and whistle in the remaining leaves and among the brittle cornstalks. They seem to be celebrating. If complex human beings feel buoyed by sunlight and even by foggy auras, we should not doubt that the birds in their immediacy and—is it simplicity?—do, too.

Later in the week, now mid-October. Another foggy morning, dew on everything as after rain. The brook, though, Angeline Brook, is pretty dry. I hear a trickle. Then two distinct, piped notes behind me. A descending minor third, up at the end of my whistling range, from the F above high C (the one above middle C— the first note children learn on the piano). I whistle it back, returning his call. Again he pipes the falling minor third, the same notes as one of the Carolina Wren calls described earlier (p. 29). But this doesn't sound like that hearty wren. I hear another similar call a couple of hundred yards away. That's his correspondent. I am merely an interloper. I speed up my walk back to where the minor third first issued. A Catbird flits across the road. Could it be? After a couple of warning sounds so prevalent in fall, there's the piped descending call. So the Catbird makes one, too, in its own timbre. Like the Titmouse and the Robin and the Carolina Wren and a legion of other birds, the Catbird sings minor thirds—but more often in fall than in spring.

As the leaves in the bright October light yellow and fall, I suspect one of the prevalent uses of birdsong diminishes. That use is deception or wily invitation to pursuit. Reflecting on the Catbird's minor third, so like several other species' calls, I wonder if this is mimicry or serendipitous duplication. What would be the advantage of mimicry or imitation? This question must occur to an apelike creature, particularly one writing a book on mimicking birdtalk.

Clearly, birdcalls have a range of survival values. Avians, who stayed in and above the trees, must have an entirely different sense of space from us creatures who descended. Most avians' sense of "flight distance," the distance at which they decide to flee or remain, is much greater than ours. Most any bird can, within five seconds of taking off, be far enough away—a few hundred yards—that we sapiens would consider it outside our lot or property or space. Any novice birder has had the experience of walking too close to, say, an American Heron—perhaps seventy yards. We were in his space before he was in ours.

Birdcalls bridge such distances for all species necessities, such as feeding, mating, and defense against predation. Birdsong, especially deceptive sound, helps birds to "hide" in broad daylight. Even non-deceptive song must share, like plumage, the purpose of survival. When a male Cardinal alights in a tree and boasts—or "yells," or "sings"—his series of descending glissandos, he may well be maneuvering to deceive predators and egg-eaters such as Sparrow Hawks and Blue Jays. His song works in tandem with his plumage to attract attention to himself. He is providing potential predators a locus of attention other than his nearby nest. So even his most earnest, boastful, upfront, "sincere" song has its deceptive intent. The implicit vanity of drawing attention to oneself seems to dominate both avians and simians. Our two species share this. A Cockatoo I know will not screech obstreperously as long as he's the center of attention. We sapiens may also draw attention, or we may drive fancy-plumaged cars or wear screechy, "loud," clothes, or we may even write.

Now, in late October, I hear amongst yellow leaves a high slurred note descending perhaps a half tone, perhaps a whole. Lots of species have a similar call. Orioles, for instance, have a flight song just like it, but an octave lower. Goldfinches make a similar call, though their timbre is thinner. Catbirds make one just like it. Searching out the source of the slurred notes, I look through binoculars across an hundred-yard field: A medium-sized hawk rises from the trees beyond. I don't hear the slurred notes again. Could it have been the hawk? Probably. The Osprey, for instance, makes almost exactly this call, but a bit higher and more piercing. Earlier I had passed within a rod of a couple of dozen Herring Gulls who ignored me in the twenty-knot breeze until I answered their high *scree*. I sucked in between my teeth, and they leapt into the air. I had ineptly called like a Hawk, probably. Sounds we are deaf to, and cries on the upper border of the human ear, commonly punctuate birdspeak. It is pretty hard to get it right, but if you don't, they flee. Birds are sensitive to mispronunciation, even more sensitive than the French. Birds have reason to be, because "mis-speak" is often their only warning of a predator, rather like passwords in wartime.

Blue Jay

# Song, Assault, or Mockery?

*W*HAT DO WE HEAR WHEN WE LISTEN to birds? What for us may seem a melodic interval may be a desperate and distressed plea. What passes as hostile assault between two Titmice (even one precipitating avian "battery" as well—pecking tailfeathers, and so on) may sound like a musical fugue. Even to call bird sounds "song" is to project a certain relatively narrow range of human activity. For birds, what we call their "songs" are more often curses and threats, defiance or concession, arrests and apprehensions, or even weather bulletins and realty leases. We simians do not tend to "sing" upon being stopped for speeding; a bird would. Nor do we "sing" when a deadly enemy approaches our home to steal and possibly eat our offspring. Or if we do sing on such occasions, we are doubtless onstage in a Greek tragedy or grand opera.

We should think a bit before we apply human behavior to birds. One way is to reverse the bird studies. Would such assessments of birds make sense if they were about us? For instance, ornithologists classify most avian behavior under territory, mating, and feeding. The brave scientists add migration, although because it is not well understood—often migratory and non-migratory branches of the same species share territory—very few studies link migration and "song." Now, if we reverse these studies, we say that most human behavior falls under social and sexual life, finding a place to live, and food. The brave sociologist or psychologist adds travel or "migration"—a fairly accurate term for American retirees flocking to Florida or Arizona.

Almost all human behavior can be reduced to such elemental necessities. Clothes and jewelry? Mating behavior. Cars, roads, and fences? Territorial determination. Agriculture, restaurants, and TV chefs? Feeding. I suppose one could subdivide the whole world economy and every separate culture into such basic categories. I feel, as a human, that such reductive classification, commonly practiced in field studies of birdsong—and arguably practiced in certain branches of anthropology and especially psychology (Maslow's "hierarchy of ends"?)—such classifying does not adequately assess *my* communications and expressions.

Mysteries abound in the songs, or the curses and threats, of birds. In his chapter "Emotions" in *The Minds of Birds,* Alexander Skutch attributes human emotions to bird vocalizations. His approach inherently questions the usual scientific assessment of birdspeak for its function or use—either to establish a mating or feeding territory, to attract (or, logically, to repel) a mate, to signal the male's readiness to take over egg incubation, and so on. Skutch notes that we human observers find or project our own emotions:

> It is remarkable how often the sounds that birds make suggest the emotions that we might feel in similar circumstances: soft notes like lullabies while calmly warming their eggs or nestlings; mournful cries while helplessly watching an intruder at their nests; harsh or grating sounds while threatening or attacking an enemy; sharp, castanet-like clacking of the bill while trying to intimidate a rival or an interloper. Birds so frequently respond to events in tones such as we might use that we suspect their emotions are similar to our own. Some birds, however, appear to lack notes appropriate for harassing occasions. (42)

That is, they have only beautiful songs! Ah, to be hemmed in and confined to beauty—to be relegated, like Midas to gold, to speak only poetry.

Skutch notes a function of birdsong identified by only a few other ornithologists, the propensity of a nesting bird such as a Flycatcher to "voice a little nest song as she passed through the doorway in the side of her bulky roofed nest and snuggled down on her two speckled eggs. Sometimes she twittered softly in the midst of a session of incubation and at intervals she called more loudly and was answered by her mate." (37) One easy way to assess birdspeak is to differentiate the bird's tone from what human speech would be in an analogous situation. For territorial calls, we may expect the human male to beat his breast, apelike, or to sing and play a rock song on amplified guitar. Or possibly the territorial call is closer to a real estate closing, with two sets of lawyers, bank reps, new owner, and so on. Somehow, the Wood Thrush and the Catbird win this comparison either way.

Reversing the analogy, what if humans could only sing beautifully, no matter the occasion? We would be living in Verdi or Donizetti or Gershwin. And who can doubt that after their silence of a cold autumn evening, birds chatter more at the advent of sunlight? No matter their various songs; they all may be singing, really expressing overflowing emotion, as if they knew *O sole mio:*

> *Che bella cosa 'e ne jurnata 'e sole,*
> *'N'aria serena dopo 'na tempesta!*
> *Per l'aria fresca pare gia 'na festa ...*
> *Che bella cosa 'e ne jurnata 'e sole!*
> (Paliotti 126)

Just over a century ago in Naples, Giovanni Capurro wrote, "What a beautiful thing it is, the daylight, the sun / In the peaceful air after a storm, / The air so clear it's like a party already, / What a beautiful thing, the sunshine"(my translation). Once Di Capua set this to music, the birds I heard this October morning could well agree. I suspect that much birdspeak is also weather-related, often seasonal, but also daily or circadian.

By the first week of November, the birds are flocking, gathering among the leafless branches "where yellow leaves or none or few do hang," as Shakespeare put it. There are Jays in abundance, a dozen here in the scrub oaks, and Robins as well, several dozen. I try out the piped descending minor third that worked a couple of weeks ago; it called a lone Jay across the parking lot. But this morning none responds. They hang together hopping among the bare branches. They do seem agitated; maybe it's their version of *Zugunruhe,* premigration restlessness. They vocalize in a kind of *chee,* also imitable by in-sucking, but lower than the Osprey. Today Robins, like the Jays, ignore my usual, burbling Robin salute. Nor do they hail each other in their characteristic calls.

I conclude that flocking and migratory birds have no use for their characteristic songs. When their behavior changes, their language changes. Their usual calls imply certain significant spaces between them; such songs might be compared to operatic passages, inappropriate in a crowded subway or taxi. Their usual songs also suggest greater individuation than during migration. Remarkably, they no longer regard calls that were answered just two weeks earlier. A comparison in human behavior might be joining the army and its attendant haircut and uniform. Birdsong functions as do civilian hair and attire, as well as property deeds.

Many birds also mimic. At least, we hear their birdtalk as imitation. Mockingbirds are named for this ability, but they are not alone in this. Blue Jays can imitate almost as well, although they don't do it from the tops of trees in rapid succession. While Mockers appear to perform gratis—thespians incarnate (or pennate)—Jays use mimicry to lurk and then to surprise their prey. Who is the better mimic, the one everyone knows is imitating, or the one we don't notice? If the Mockingbird delights like an actor or even a parodist, the Blue Jay, like a double agent, prefers the shadows. He talks clandestinely in several bird dialects.

One mid-February morning in a dusting of snow, I heard an apparent Carolina Wren repeat a grace note and descending minor third. Looking for the bird typically halfway up some leafless bush, I could not find it. After several exchanges, I finally saw a Blue Jay low to the ground. Once I saw it, it made a guttural *caw* like a small Crow. In *Bird Sounds*, Barry MacKay comments on such Jay ability, and on the nature of mimicry.

> Blue Jays have a call that is similar to that of Red-Tailed Hawks. Whether or not this derives from true mimicry, the cry so closely resembles that of the raptor that some birders do not assume that a hawk's call actually comes from a hawk until they see the hawk make the call. (MacKay 46)

Blue Jays, then, make a wide variety of non-Jay calls. Many of these apparently deceive, like duck hunters *quack*ing from a blind.

When are similar songs true mimicry? The story of bird mimicry does not begin and end with deception and parody. This book started with a wide variety of birds making similar sounds and intervals—descending minor thirds, ascending fourths, glissandos. Would it be too much to call this the lingua franca of the species? It may well turn out that certain sounds are universally recognized among birds. Surely their warnings, the fricative *chuck-chucks* and in-sucking lisps, are clear even to simians. What then can they make of each others' descending minor thirds? Do they function like stone walls in New England? Or like answering the phone? They do seem to hold a function quite beyond any imitation or mockery.

Magpie

# Auspices:
# Roman & Native American

*W*E HUMANS HAVE ALWAYS TURNED TO birds, to their flight patterns and their songs, for signs and portents. Ancient and prehistoric people observed birds to prepare for the future, as much as seeking among the counseling stars and voices in the wind. Their "future" could have been the next hour, the day ahead, or a lifetime. By Roman times, just at the start of the Empire, one member of the college of augurs, Marcus Tullius Cicero lamented how the last ten years had seen the decline of consultation of bird signs, the auspices. In *De Divinatione,* Cicero's brother Quintus contrasts Roman neglect with the greater piety in the outlying provinces of Pamphylia, Pisidia, Lycia, and especially Cilicia, where the Cicero brothers were Roman governors.

> Quae quidem nunc a Romanis auguribus ignorantur ... a Cilicibus, Pamphyliis, Pisidis, Lyciis tenentur. (Cicero 252)

While Cicero governed Cilicia with his brother's assistance, they met and befriended King Deiotarus of Lesser

Armenia and Gallograecia. Making the argument for auspices, Cicero's brother cites this ruler from the mountain regions. King Deiotarus always consulted the auspices—the avian augurs—before and even during a trip. Several times he stopped his travels because of the auspices. Once he returned home because of the flight of an eagle. The next day, the room that he was scheduled to stay in collapsed.

Both birdsong and birdflight have been considered premonitory. Perhaps Shakespeare depends upon such ideas when, for instance, Juliet and Romeo debate whether it is the Nightingale or the Lark who sings and presages Romeo's arrest.

Jul.  It was the nightingale, and not the lark
      That pierc'd the fearful hollow of thine ear;
      Nightly she sings on yond pomegranate tree:
      Believe me, love, it was the nightingale.

Rom. It was the lark, the herald of the morn,
      No nightingale: look, love, what envious streaks
      Do lace the severing clouds in yonder east ... (3.5)

Then Romeo accedes to Juliet's desire that he stay. With bravado, he says he is content to be captured, even to die, if that is her will. Like Petruchio, who misnames the irksome Kate a fair and modest maid, Romeo misnames the bird, "Nor that is not the lark, whose notes do beat / The vaulty heaven so high above our heads." But such mis-identification could be fatal for Romeo, two lines later, "Come, death, and welcome!" Then

54

Juliet awakens to their danger, foreboded by the correct song identification,

> It is the lark that sings so out of tune,
> Straining harsh discords and unpleasing sharps.
> Some say the lark makes sweet division;
> This doth not so, for she divideth us. (3.5.26ff.)

Juliet's "field I.D." of the lark is well expressed, though she might say the same for Messiaen. The beautiful song of the lark here warns the lovers, as elsewhere in the canon, in *MacBeth*, the freedom-loving Purple Martin ("martlet") greets the King entering the castle where he will die.

> This guest of summer,
> The temple-haunting martlet, does approve
> By his loved mansionry that the heavens' breath
> Smells wooingly here. (1.6.3–6)

To the naive observer of feather headdresses, dances, and birdcalls, aboriginal cultures are most engaged in the cross-species encounter I discuss. Birds are entwined in so much tribal lore. Although Native American encyclopedias often do not include an entry for "bird," when they do, it is often a translation of a family name. When I look up birds species, such as Crow, Eagle and Owl in *The Encyclopedia of Native American Religions,* I find more proper names—David W. Owl, a Cherokee Baptist minister whose parish was among the Seneca on the Cattaraugus Reservation; Adam

Fortunate Eagle, one of the activist occupiers of Alca-
traz Island for nineteen months beginning in 1969.
(Hirschfelder 205; Hoxie 13) Clearly, birds are so central to native peoples that tribal subdivisions, moieties,
or "houses"—and even families—take on bird names.
A recent biography follows Zintkala Nuni, also known
as *The Lost Bird of Wounded Knee.* (Renée Flood)

In William Fenton's article "North Iroquoian Culture Patterns," a seventeenth century French document
records copies of native—probably Seneca—pic-
tographs of family totems of those in a war party. Each
beast holds a war club, axe, or knife. After the Turtle,
Wolf, Bear, Beaver, Deer, and Wild Potato (!) come the
Large Snipe, Small Snipe, and Hawk (with club, knife,
and axe, respectively). (Fenton 299) Counsels are represented by totem animals with mouths open in apparent conversation—a multiplication of our theme of
cross-species communiqués. Some family names reflect
such species mixes—for example, Henry and Mary
Crow Dog. (Sturtevant, vol. 13: 990–94)

But ethnomusicology comes to our rescue. William
Powers' study of Lakota sacred language establishes
the primacy of Native Americans in cross-species communication. One of the sacred Oglala languages can
be used with nonhumans.

> It is believed that a number of animals and birds
> can communicate with common people and medi-
> cine men and that frequently these nonhuman species
> speak in Lakota. The communication between

humans and nonhumans occurs most frequently during the vision Quest. Under ritual conditions, virtually every species is capable of speaking to the medicine man in Lakota—buffalo, deer, elk, coyotes, wolves, snakes, and so forth.

Sometimes the animal or bird is capable of signaling the medicine men in the species's natural utterances, for example, the howl of a wolf, the bark of a coyote, the hoot of an owl, and the crowing of a cock, all of which are interpreted as omens of death particularly if the sounds are heard during an inappropriate time of day or night for that animal or bird to be active. Most often, communication between people and animals occurs in the vision Quest, Sweat Lodge, or in the Yuwipi. (Powers, W. 26)

Interesting how time of day, chronobiology, factors into the meaning of animal sounds. Messiaen would heartily agree, as we see later ("North Atlantic Birds," p. 124).

I would argue that many of the difficulties early musicologists found in notating Native American songs crop up in birdsong as well, from quarter tones and other surprising intervals to glissandos and slurred effects. In one early, elsewhere wrongheaded attempt, Frederick Burton makes at least one point of agreement:

There is much vagueness in the Indian's frequent slurring from one note to another, the intervals are often, to say the least, unexpected, their scale relationship hard to determine until long familiarity with both

57

> style of songs and performance enables one to lis-
> ten in much the same spirit with which the song is
> sung. (F. Burton 22)

Birdtalkers must concentrate and adapt their ears much
as ethnomusicologists learned to in their field studies.
I have only started to hear quarter tones after years of
trying to notate avian intervals, years of finding my
transcriptions inadequate.

In William Powers' chapter "Naming the Sacred,"
we find that the Lakota make at least four distinctions
to our two regarding Golden Eagles and Bald Eagles,
adding specific names for immature Bald and immature Golden. The Lakota also associate certain birds
with certain hunted animals, for example, the Swallow
and the Black-tail Deer, the Crow and the White-tail
Deer. At the same time, certain birds are harbingers of
specific seasons—the Crow, of spring; the Swallow, of
fall. The Magpie announces winter, the Meadowlark,
summer. (148–52)

Rhode Island's founder, Roger Williams, in his *Key into
the Language of America,* records some of the Narragansett language for birds in 1643. In his chapter "Of
Fowle," after the word for Eagle *(Wompissacuk)* he
records those for Turkeys *(Neyhom),* Partridges, Heath-
cocks and especially Blackbirds *(Chogan, euck):*

> Of this sort there be millions, which are great
> devourers of the *Indian* corne as soon as it appears

out of the ground; Unto this sort of Birds, especially may the mysticall Fowles, the Divells be well resembled (and so it pleaseth the Lord Jesus himselfe to observe, *Matth.13*. which mystical Fowle follow the sowing of the Word, and pick it up from loose and carelesse heareres, as these Black-birds follow the material feed. (Williams 89)

Williams records that the Narragansetts would post their biggest children in "little watch-houses in the middle of their fields ... early in the morning [to] prevent the Birds." But they would not harm Crows *(Kaukont tuock)* because of lore:

Scarce one *Native* amongst an hundred wil kil them because they have a tradition, that the Crow brought them at first *Indian* Graine of Corne in one Eare, and an *Indian* or *French* Beane in another, from the Great God *Kautantouwits* field in the Southwest from whence they hold came all their Corne and Beanes. (Williams 90)

The Narragansett word for "Goose" is onomatopoetic, *Honck* or plural, *honckock*. They loved hunting ducks, looked forward to using European guns for that purpose.

On other birds besides Crows, similar unwritten stories enter into cross-cultural—or in our case, cross-species—encounters. In his book on *The California Indians,* Heizer tells of ceremonial sacrifice of Condors and Eagles, and the use of bird parts in many ceremonies. (124) Note that the most feared bird of all, among several California tribes, is the Western Meadowlark. I would hazard this fear derives from its voice and song—beautiful, varied, and penetrating. Even if one does not believe in spirits, the Meadowlark seems to bear a message from another world. For us, that world is Birdworld.

Like good Nineteenth-Century naturalists, the Narragansetts hunted and ate most all fowl, even our misnamed, onomastic Buzzards Bay Cormorants *(Kitsuog)*. Roger Williams tells us their method: "These they take in the night time, where they are asleepe on rocks, off at Sea, and bring in at break of day great store of them." (91) Among other bird lore, Williams reports the Narragansett bird name *Sachem:*

> ... a little Bird about the bignesse of a swallow, or lesse, to which the *Indians* give that name, because of its *Sachim* or Princelike courage and Command over greater Birds, that a man shall often see this small Bird pursue and put to flight the Crow, and other birds farre bigger then it selfe. (Williams 92)

In our time the birds most likely to be chasing Crows are Purple Martins and others in the Blackbird family. I have seen them also chase Red-Tailed Hawks. Williams quotes the word-phrase *Sowwanakitauwaw* for "they are going southward," when the "Geese and other Fowle at the approach of winter betake themselves in admirable Order and discerning their Course even all the night long." (92)

As for songbirds, they are largely beneath Williams' survivalist notice, "There are abundance of singing Birds whose names I have little as yet inquired after." (92) However, he does conclude, as I have *pace* St. Francis, that birds teach *us* a kind of gratitude or "natural piety":

> How sweetly doe all the severall sorts of Heavenly Birds, in all Coasts of the World, preach unto Men the prayse of their Makers Wisdome, Power, and Goodnesse, who feedes them and their young ones Summer and Winter ... although they neither sow nor reape, nor gather into Barnes. (93)

Williams concludes his chapter on birds as he does his others, with an hymn, this one in part,

> If man provide eke for his Birds,
>     In Yard, in Coops, in Cage.
> And each Bird spends in songs and tunes,
>     His little time and Age! (93)

*Mockingbird*

# The Supreme Mocker

*E*AGLES, WINGS SCULPTED OPEN, perch atop the two flagpoles in front of the U.S. Supreme Court. Ben Franklin would have preferred a departure from that avian symbol of empire; he nominated the Turkey for national bird. I had never seen a Wild Turkey in flight until this year—two rising from a rural road, a magnificent sight, rather like the takeoff of a C-130.

But back to D.C. On summer days those Supreme Court flagpoles host another avian on top of one eagle: here sits the court jester, a Mockingbird. I whistle back the intervals and appogiaturas, the descending minor thirds, the demiquavers of his grabbag of melody: the Cardinal's descending sixth glissando, the Carolina Wren's "Mexican Hat Dance" theme. No Thrush song this morning, so perhaps he observes some diurnal decorum. Wood Thrushes usually complete their full song in the evening. Pentatonic, it is the same scale as the blues. Many bird notes, like blue notes, fall between two diatonic notes. When Thrushes sing the blues, they sound like Stan Getz were he to play the flute. The notes float and sail.

My East Capitol Street Mocker leaps vertically in the air above his eagle perch, helicopters for a couple of seconds and displays his white wing stripes, then settles back on the finial eagle's wing. Though feathered of metal, the eagle and he are about the same size. The Mocker's look-ma-no-hands wing display completes our introduction: He has warned me. I'm in his space. Has he noticed my broad-brimmed hat, and beneath it a giant nestling, no master of flight? His "word-hoard," as the Anglo-Saxons called it, comprises a vast anthology of other birds' calls, done in his own timbre, sometimes with his own added microtones. It is relatively easy to whistle back to Mockingbirds; if you can't repeat one of their stolen songs, try another. The one I have called the Cardinal's descending sixth usually has a blue note or microtone grace note so it sounds like a triplet.

Most Mockingbirds have a couple of dozen songs within the range of human—read *my*—whistling. (Contrast Redwinged Blackbirds, with their lovely filigree of ultrasonic squeaks.)

Staying out of that Mockingbird's territory is not a problem since I am wingless, and moreover, settled in the air-conditioned Folger Shakespeare Library. My whole training as an academic has been territorial, to keep off others' academic turf. So I know the message, although I have trespassed often—into journalism for the *New York Times Magazine,* an Oscar-nominated film, folklore, Italian Risorgimento history, even the history of science and medicine, and of course American literature, though my training is in Renaissance English. Journals and conference directors have often greeted me with the academic equivalent of "Keep out of my tree!" Only my talented, multivocal, polysemous academic mentors manage to sneak across disciplines with ease.

On a visit to Monticello, as I leave the confines of the all-weather passage and the south pavilion, I hear another Mocker. Less multivocal than the Supreme Mocker, this one has the whole giant garden and the orchard beyond to himself. The heat of the day, high nineties, has peaked and passed. This Mockingbird does not mimic snippets of Thrush. Mostly he pipes a minor third, two notes in rapid succession, like a Titmouse only more nervous.

I echo back my version of his song. He adds another three or four riffs. I add my version of them, too. Where is he? Something shoots out of a fruit tree, and as it swerves I see the mocking stripes. He measures out his area, or he leaves it to me. Have I won the field? Hard to say, since it is no longer mating season.

My stay at the Folger over, I pause at a rest stop on the New Jersey Pike. Cars unload their passengers, swimming in August heat. I take the plunge. The desolate pavement exudes waves of hot air, the trash bins fill with cups from soft drinks that have sustained life between Hightstown and New Brunswick. Two youths sleep in the backseat of the maroon car parked, windows open, next to me. My dulled mind lifts, surprised by a wordy Mocker-locutor who hails from a maple tree bordering a field that abuts the gas plaza. I try to whistle back, but my lips are parched. I sound like a child learning to whistle. A passing couple look at me.

Should I explain? "Oh, I really *can* whistle, I can too. I do it all the time, mainly to Robins, Titmice, Cardinals, Orioles, and Mockingbirds. There's one over in that grove. Hear that? No, there really *is* one. I'm not bananas." I let them pass by unenlightened—and myself unexposed. I manage a couple of phrases in Mockerese—or mockeries. When I return from Roy Rodgers with my coffee, the bird has flown.

Even here amidst the asphalt smell and the gas pumps, the paper cups and brimming bins, nature takes its late-twentieth-century stand. The birdsong, not to mention the "birdalog," transforms the dire necessities—gas, oil and water for the car, other liquids and facilities for the body. If I were to lead a movement—D.C. makes one think politically—it would be for talking to birds in urban and highway environs which we have created and which they do not entirely disdain. Most of what we say to each other in species encounters may be on the order of "fashion statements." Look at me. No, *me*. But some of it is on the order of much human conversation: "Nice day, 'nt it?" Or Lennon and McCartney's "Here Comes the Sun." And *"O sole mio!"*

As I get in my car, I notice the fellows are no longer sleeping in the next. They have flown, too. I stand cheered, rested, by this rest stop, more by the bird than all the rest—pun intended. Shakespeare calls the Lark's morningsong "hymns at heaven's gate." (Sonnet 29) I recall also that wonderful passage of throwaway verse late in the *Merchant of Venice* when, awaiting Portia's return, Jessica complains, "I am never merry when I hear sweet music." Lorenzo psychologizes, analyzes:

> The reason is, your spirits are attentive.
> For do but note a wild and wanton herd
> Or race of youthful and unhandled colts . . .
> If they but hear perchance a trumpet sound,
> Or any air of music touch their ears,
> You shall perceive them make a mutual stand,
> Their savage eyes turned to a modest gaze
> By the sweet power of music. . . . (5.1.70ff.)

The passage goes on to become famous, with its more invidious lines against those who do not appreciate music: "The man that hath no music in himself, / Nor is not moved by concord of sweet sounds, / Is fit for treason, stratagems, and spoils ... / Let no such man be trusted." Following Lorenzo (or Shakespeare), I urge that those who fail to whistle to birds not be allowed to vote, or to drive, to bear arms. Take your pick. Barring such stipulations, I shall continue to organize the nondenominational Society of St. Francis of the Gas Plazas.

*Goldfinch*

# From Guns to Birdfeeders

*T*HE TWENTIETH CENTURY SAW an enormous change in attitudes toward birdlife. The first decades witnessed a burgeoning of ornithological studies, but often as an extension of hunting and capture. A reader of the *Auk's* predecessor, the *Bulletin of the Nuttall Ornithological Club,* for 1882 is greeted with one Dr. Merriam's cheering account of a social occasion in the service of ornithology.

> One rainy afternoon about the middle of July, while the Judge was catching salmon at the famous "Upper Pool" on the Godbout, Mr. Nap. A. Comeau and I climbed a high and densely wooded hill that rises from the western border of the pool, and when near the summit saw a Pine Grosbeak, in the slate and golden plumage, hopping about among the branches of a large Balsam *(Abies balsamea)*. I was within twenty feet from the bird, but having only a rifle was unable to secure it. (121)

To "secure" has an ominous tone for the modern reader, for, like his predecessor John James Audubon, Dr. Merriam meant to collect it as a specimen by shooting it.

In this case, he missed. His companion did not, for, following the physician's example, "He has since written me that he has shot several after I left." This serves me as an admonition. Writers on birds inevitably desire to share their often solitary, inevitably hermit-like pursuit. Their readers may not share their proclivities — for instance, killing it to save it.

My own interest, too, can be seen as an intrusion, a mucking-up of natural order. When at my best as an avian mimic, I may be like a decoy Puffin placed on an island to attract released nestlings back to a former site. My "answering calls" may confuse the territorial males, and the females as well. What if I attracted more females than the real birds? That would be a reproductive and genetic disaster. Fortunately, that has not happened. I seem to attract only males, and only at their most territorial.

Why do this? Perhaps it is the monkey or the mocker in me. Perhaps it is the idealist, perhaps the nostalgic. The idealist wants to break barriers between species, the nostalgic wants to connect with nature as in childhood when, according to Wordsworth, we were closer to nature and to God. But most likely I echo birds as a linguist and musician. I have studied languages, European Romance and Slavic, much of my life, although my training is literary. I have spent hours, whole days, some years slogging through various texts that require dictionaries. I enjoy learning what I do not know, especially when veiled in a language I can but partially construe. For many years I have been an amateur jazz musician, even the composer of a few jazz tunes, some based on Wood Thrush and Oriole songs. So this book is a prelexical approach to a dictionary of bird language—confining ourselves to the minority of sounds imitable by us—or really, by me.

Essentially, imitating bird call notes is like imitating a telephone dial tone. A connection has been made. That is it. In his book on English Robins, David Lack makes this point.

> Analysis of the sound-tracks of bird song has shown that most small birds include in their songs notes of a frequency well above the limits to which the human ear is sensitive, so that a bird's song probably does not sound the same to another bird as it does to us. (34)

Mr. Lack seems to forget this wider range of avian perception when he notes the prevalence of both female and male English Robin singing in the autumn:

> In this season not only the cocks but also about half of the hen robins sing, their song being indistinguishable from that of the cocks. (34)

I am sure that the birds can tell the difference easily. The future of the species depends on it.

It may also depend on not landing in Maurice's backyard. Enthusiastically recounting the great White Goose Festival along the St. Lawrence River, our host Maurice tells of the sky white with Geese, and getting his shotgun to provide supper. I always recommend Konrad Lorenz to Goose hunters; Lorenz's *King Solomon's Ring* recounts his experiences with Geese who mate for life, their young bonding with humans should they lose a parent.

Even if you have no interest in extending your parenting role into the avian sphere, more good reasons exist to call birds—or rather, to return birds' calls. Birds are tasteful conversationalists. They do not talk about digestion in restaurants, nor about flatulence, though all those seeds and berries must do something. They do not converse about their health problems, about Dr. Bierstein's latest discovery from the blood test and his consequent recommendation of which trendy drug you've seen advertised on TV. Nor do birds talk at great length about sports teams in their sumptuous new stadiums, about the latest contract negotiated by this knuckleballer or that quarterback. The stadiums they evaluate only as nesting sites. The newer ones are often worse, hostile to birds and far from wild fruiting bushes and other feed—except mosquitoes and bugs. Plenty of those, though the electric zappers are eliminating food supply there. Birds' stock portfolios are remarkably thin, although some few species do hoard, and their discussion of investments can be summed up in the seasonal ebb and flow of sunlight. They do chatter a great deal about weather, and rains cause many to sink into silence. Not the Robins, though. Even among humans, the avian ability to discuss weather instead of serious subjects has always been a sign of good breeding. And birds are nothing if not good breeders. The migratory species would probably watch the weather channel before migration if they knew human language. Certainly butterflies should, too. When Hurricane Bob tore through Rhode Island at 110 mph, I saw dozens of Monarchs caught in their migration swept backward at very high speeds.

In fact, I suspect birds have their own weather channel, or at the least, weather reports. Late October I heard around sunrise very rapid sixteenth-note triplets, an ascending minor third: C sharp, D, E: CDECDE CDECDE. Two beats a second, twelve notes a second. This was a familiar Carolina Wren call, but faster than I have heard it. Perhaps the speed reflected the temperature. The astronomer Harlow Shapley once created an accurate thermometer from ants because their speed varied as did the temperature. In the case of ants, they were the opposite of humans, walking faster in the heat, slower in cold. I think birdsong contrarily speeds up in cold weather. The Carolina Wren's late October morning song is essentially a weather report. But below a certain temperature, there are few such reports. Or any other news from birds.

Finally, birds do not bemoan or complain about their work, although they certainly could. They search all day, every day to find food and to avoid predators. They could heap a torrent of abuse on their interlocutors. Swallows surely demonstrate great energy at dusk

sweeping across fields for flies and gnats to swallow—
pun intended. Robins watch eagerly with their characteristic head-tilt, hour upon hour, for those worms.
Chickadees gather seeds off trees, Goldfinch thistle
seed, off August driveways if necessary. Essentially
trapped in the hunter-gatherer stage of cultural evolution, birds spend the long daylight hours, every waking moment, looking for food. At least, the oscine
passerines do. Their search for seeds and fruits and
bugs must work out about even in calorie intake versus
expenditure. And when they're feeding young, they fall
behind. Any mother Robin or Cardinal looks frantic
and thin about ten days into her twelve-to-fourteen-
day nesting cycle. The males look frantic, too, among
species where both feed the young. Fish-eaters, such as
Osprey, Kingfisher, Heron, and Eagle, seem to have
slightly more "free time" just to soar. Or maybe that
is just my human perception based on our species' prej-
udice in favor of a protein-rich diet.

Such observations and appreciations grew out of
the twentieth century, which brought us from
Audubon's shoot-and-sketch approach to birdlife. Perhaps the twenty-first century will bring us into a conversational acquaintance with our airborne rivals.

As surely as the nineteenth century saw the growth
of the capture model of bird study, it also fostered some
wonderful "natural piety," to borrow Wordsworth's
phrase. For instance, in France, historian and journal-

ist Jules Michelet wrote a lovely book toward the end of his life, a retreat from the *sujet humaine*. He contrasts his book *L'Oiseau* to his predecessor Tousenels', which is pervaded with the *vocation militaire du Lorrain*. (Michelet 9) His own is a book of peace, against hunting, *"en haine de la chasse."* (9) He promises to avoid his mentor's human analogies, his continual personifications, a device common among writers on birds—a fate not entirely avoided by myself.

In rejecting the usual nineteenth-century hunt-capture-and-classify approach, Michelet accepts the gender taunt that his approach is dreamy and feminine. That the heart of a woman is mixed in his book, Michelet says, "we accept as praise," *("Nous acceptons comme un' éloge").* (10) In his chapter on song, Michelet writes a vivid hymn to the birds,

> Winged voices, voices of fire, voices of angels, emanations of an intense life superior to ours, of a life voyaging and mobile, which bequeaths to the laborer tied to his furrow thoughts more serene and a dream of liberty. (256)

He continues in this elevated vein a rapturous encomium. The greatest spectacle in nature is the "leaves and flowers of its silent (spring) concert, its song of March and April, its symphony of May." Michelet emphasizes that birds lived before mankind, but not mankind without birds; that birds protect humans from many insects; that the laborer's bird, in humble dress, is the Lark. If his is an archaic style, nostalgia might call it more than adequate for its subject.

Any modern student of birdsong must be dazzled by the ever increasing scientific literature of bird vocalizations. Donald Kroodsma and Edward Miller have collected some prominent essays, as had R. A. Hinde a quarter-century before. Many of these studies offend the squeamish or the sensitive. For a German study reported in 1960 in *Behavior,* Turkeys were surgically deafened. Although they brooded on the eggs until they hatched, they then killed their young presumably for their lack of the familiar *peep*ing bond. (Schleidt 254) In a more famous instance of surgery to isolate the sources of birdsong, Fernando Nottebohm sectioned the tracheosyringeal branch of the hypoglossal nerve of the male canary. This is no minor surgery; the birds are nearly muted when it's the left syringeal nerve. Or to see whether birds harbor inborn "templates" of songs, or if they learn their songs by hearing them, a scientist may remove the cochlea from several birds, rendering them deaf. Such laboratory procedures reveal the anatomy and biology of birdsong, for instance, the role of the medulla. Nottebohm includes a photograph of a cross-section of a male canary medulla showing the *commissura infima,* which joins right and left halves of the medulla at the level of the tracheosyringealis part of the hypoglossal nucleus. If you can say that last phrase three times fast, you can imitate any birdsong in this book.

Recently *The New Yorker* portrayed Nottebohm's and Ofer Tchernichovski's researches on mapping the changes in Canary brains as they (the birds, not Nottebohm and Tchernichovski) learn to sing. They place month-old Canaries in a sound-studio cage with a plastic daddyo wired for song. If a researcher whistles Gershwin, the plastic bird can imitate it, though "Gershwin is a bit too complex for a songbird to master," according to Michael Specter. Perhaps. I have heard passerine songs more complex than Gershwin melodies, however—those of Orioles, Redwings and Starlings, Wood Thrushes, Mockingbirds, and certain Warblers. More discouraging for our purpose is the inducement offered Nottebohm's birds for learning. The senior scientist says, "Now, if we want to say a certain note was learned at a certain instant, we can take the bird and sacrifice it the second we see him learn that note." (Specter 53) Somehow, except for suicidal canaries, being "sacrificed" doesn't seem the best inducement for learning.

Despite great advances in knowledge of avian neurology, and similar advances in bird behavior studies, we still can only guess at how birds use their songs or language. Even to call it a "song" is to misrepresent what may sometimes be more like spitting than singing. A human behavior comparable to territorial birdsong may be the Western film cliche of the gunfighter hitching up his gun belt. As for the usual scientific experiments, one involves playing bird songs back to the birds that made them. If the birds are at all like adolescent human would-be rock stars, they enjoy hearing themselves recorded. But often the experimenters are more rigorous and unforgiving. It's a wonder they don't drive the birds wacko. Such scientific articles often have pictures of the recorded bird—say, a starling—standing atop the irritant speaker box, giving it hell.

The nineteenth century capture model of ornithology may have grown into such modern scientific study where we murder to dissect. It also resulted in federal laws, the first being the Migratory Bird Treaty Act of 1918, part of international action to halt the decline in migratory bird population:

> The primary threat to migratory bird populations when the Act was passed was unrestrained shooting for commerce and sport. Consequently, the main thrust of the Act and the treaty [with Canada] is to regulate "taking" of migratory birds, especially hunting. (Bean 64)

In one case resulting from Congress's act, *Missouri vs. Holland* (1920), comes the stark prediction, "But for the treaty and the statute there might soon be no birds for any powers to deal with." (Bean 63) Later federal laws (1940 and 1992) have protected the Eagle, with exceptions for Native American religious practices. (Bean 465)

*Wood Thrush*

# Avitherapy

YOU CAN TALK TO YOUR FRIENDS, or, if you have no friends enthralled by details of your latest body fluid samples and intestinal problems, you can talk to a physician—who is usually too busy to listen after a couple of minutes. If your problems are more pressing, you can talk to a psychiatrist.

Or you can talk to a bird.

Birds charge less—considerably less. And their conversation is more beautiful, even if your shrink is operatic. Birds won't shower you with jargon based on bad translations. (Freud never used the term "ego," for example, which came in with the 1933 English translation.) Avian language may well be the language of the *psyche,* of the soul and mind.

A good reader of my book must have inferred by now that birdtalkers have found the cheapest therapy. I do not deny it. In fact, in discussions with bird enthusiasts I have found that their interest often grew fastest during a period of personal crisis. Some wonderful ornithological works also acknowledge the sanative effect of birds, especially birdsong. Quite often books on birds are departures, the culmination of academic careers in other disciplines, such as the emeritus psychologist Harold Burtt's *The Psychology of Birds.*

Consider the nineteenth century French popular historian Jules Michelet, cited in the previous chapter. For forty years (from 1833 to 1872) he published twenty-seven volumes in the history of France from the Middle Ages to 1815. Born the son of a printer imprisoned for debt in 1808 when young Michelet was ten, Jules thrived as a student and eventually became a history teacher at *École normale supérieur,* and later at the Collège de France. Suspended at the revolution of 1848, reinstated under the Second Republic in March, suspended anew two years later, his permanent dismissal followed a year later when he refused to take the loyalty oath to the Empire. (Guthrie 229) After such treatment at the hands of his fellow beings, and after lifelong study of their even worse treatment of each other—called "history"—is it any wonder Michelet found solace in the birds?

He says as much in his preface to *L'Oiseau,* "How the Author was Led to the Study of Nature." He feels he owes his faithful public, who have not abandoned him over such a long time, the private circumstances that led him to "hatching" this book—"if it is a book." He implies it may be an egg, one overseen by his collaborative friends and especially his other collaborators (nesting Swallow, flitting Red-breast and Nightingale)—*les hirondelles familières ... le rouge-gorge domestiques ... et parfois le rossignol.* (Michelet 4)

> The heavy times, the life, the work, violent changes of our age, the exile from the intelligentsia among whom we lived, nothing has replaced. The hard work of history finds relaxation in teaching, which complements it. The interruption of that left only silence. To whom look for relaxation and moral refreshment, if not to nature? (Michelet 4)

The eighteenth century alone contains a "thousand years of combat" from which Bernadin de Saint-Pierre recovers with the touching words of Ramond, "So many irreparable losses wept for on the breast of nature!" As for Michelet, he looks for other consolation than solitary tears and sayings which sweeten the wounded heart, "We seek a stimulant cordial to keep moving forward, a restorative sip from an inexhaustible source, a new force, one with wings!" (Michelet 5) And Jules Michelet is not alone.

Others have found nonhuman succor in nature. In literature, Jonathan Swift's Gulliver returns home after his fourth voyage to the land of the philosopher-horses, the Houyhnhnms. Gulliver precedes us in cross-species conversation. After months of talking to the high-minded horses, he grows disgusted with human behavior and human language. The Houyhnhnms, you recall, had no word for "lying." Rational creatures, they could see no reason for language except to express truth.

Probably the most famous turning to birds in the midst of personal crisis is John Keats's "Ode to a

Nightingale." Despairing over the loss of his younger brother, and over the wasted, indifferent beauty of the spring morning that surrounds him, Keats feels drugged as if by hemlock or opium. At first hearing the Nightingale he feels he wants to fly like that creature, but as he listens he finds himself envious of the bird as singer. The bird has a kind of impersonal immortality in his song, more or less the same as it has been since the days of the biblical Ruth. The bird has achieved what Keats looks for, a song that lives on through Negative Capability, where will and personality are replaced by art. Keats's depression has been treated by avitherapy.

Moving from literature to real life, take the example of a returning student of mine, the mother of five. Married to a dependable husband with artistic training, she and her whole family once became stranded in a snowstorm in an isolated cabin in Canada. An accompanying friend who did not take off her hooded jacket for three days, even in the cabin, asked at one point, "Why are we doing this?" My student's husband began shaking—at first, apparently from the cold. But upon seeking the nearest physician, they found out he was suffering a nervous breakdown. The physician recommended visiting family—in Arizona? or Hawaii? They did. (Shall we call it the Italian cure?) Ever afterward, my student recalled the White-throated Sparrows on the birdtray out the window at the motel where the family recovered from the freezing cabin. And then she remembered the beautiful songs of the stunning

Cardinals out the window of their cousin's cozy ranch house. Simple pleasures. And health restored through birdtalk.

Birds speak theatrically, as do we who respond to them. Humans gather closer together to communicate. Usually we speak at less than the distance of our own height. Birds, on the other hand, mount a scaffold or climb a bell-tower. The highest tree. To humans, they all seem to be would-be politicians at national conventions. But that is not entirely true; even their common conversation takes place over substantial distances. So birdtalkers self-dramatize. Such self-projection is a common ploy in other forms of therapy. Clear the air. Wave your arms (or wings). It's good for you.

You have a choice of avitherapists, just as you do psychologists and psychotherapists. I began with that most cheering and practical of advisors, the American Robin. He's a burbler and a bubbler, rather impure, not flutelike. Insistent and repetitive, but varied, his overall advice is cheery and direct. Do this. You can do it. Get at it. Don't delay. I think of him as a saxophonist, but not the lilting Paul Desmond or Stan Getz. Robins are closer to the rock and roll saxophonist.

If you suffer from obsessive compulsions, you have two choices. You can birdtalk to a truly obsessive species, such as the Titmouse. (See the philosopher Hartshorne on many species that have a low monotony threshold!) Or you may choose one of the great riffing species who never seem to repeat. The Mockingbird is an obvious choice here; others include Red-winged Blackbirds and Warblers.

For bipolar problems, you can choose a truly conflicted bird such as the Woodcock, who on the ground sounds like a large buzzing insect and in the air like a hundred kisses. Or you might be better off with a steady-Eddy sort White-throated Sparrow.

Depressives have a wide range of options. Almost any birdsong takes one outside oneself into the world of a creature so small, yet so present. In America, depressives are more fortunate than John Keats, for we have the most beautiful of singers, the Wood Thrush. Its pentatonic tunes, which modulate surprisingly from key to key, suggest melancholy, but they also suggest almost total bliss. Less blissful, the Mourning Dove sounds dignified, almost funereal, although he may be having the time of his life. Depressives who talk with Mourning Doves may find a perfect "objective correlative" for their interior feeling.

## Robin

# Literary Birds

*S*OME OF THE WORST LINES in English poetry were inspired by birds. Consider Shelley's infamous "Bird thou never wert" and Emily Dickinson's "But were I Cuckoo born" (when my students usually think she was born cuckoo). Yet even this unfortunate line, a line which colloquial anachronism has killed—as it has W. B. Yeats's favorite adjective, "gay"—even Dickinson's fatal line appears in one of her half-dozen fine poems on Robins. She also has famous poems on the Hummingbird and the golden Baltimore Oriole ("One of the ones that Midas Touched"). Birds have elicited some of the best lines, too—in Keats, in Shakespeare, in Catullus, in Vergil, and in Yeats, to name a few. Many of these bird references are exalted, but we start with the humble.

Dickinson's Robin poems rank as definitive. Her Robin is a metaphor for the New England farmer, even the working classes, and a spokesman for conventional values. I start with her later verse, in reverse order of composition:

The Robin is a Gabriel
>    In humble circumstances—
His Dress denotes him socially,
>    Of Transport's Working Classes—
He has the punctuality
>    Of the New England Farmer—
The same oblique integrity,
>    A Vista vastly warmer—
(Dickinson, no. 1483)

We can hear Dickinson's own nineteenth-century New England dialect in this last line of the first stanza (or first two stanzas in ballad form). She would have said, "a vistah vahstly wahmah." This I hypothesize from the early pronunciation of the place-name, "Amherst." A teacher of mine who came to Amherst in 1928, Theodore Baird, had it from a colleague who had arrived in the waning years of the nineteenth century, when Calvin Coolidge was the College valedictorian. Amherst was then pronounced *Amst.*

More than a dozen years before she wrote this almost Whitmanesque idea celebrating Gabriel Robin's social class, Dickinson wrote one epigrammatic stanza:

The Robin for the Crumb
>    Returns no syllable
But long records the Lady's name
>    In silver Chronicle. (Dickinson, no. 864)

Earlier that year—a couple of years after her *annus*

*mirabilis* of 1862—she interprets the Robin's silence and renders its songbursts precisely:

> The Robin is the One
> That interrupt the Morn
> With hurried—few—express Reports
> When March is scarcely on—
> (Dickinson, no. 828)

That's it. Dickinson here lays down the best description of the American Robin's song, a burbling, impure but emphatic series. Most people over a certain age— six years in the suburbs, ten in the cities?—can identify a Robin when they see one, but how many know it by its song? Far fewer. One in a hundred, a thousand. Yet its song is unmistakable. And it sings during light rain, unlike many other birds. This pluvial singing St. Francis would approve, its grace before meals.

"The Robin is the One," is what Yeats calls "passionate syntax," a poetic thwarting of the limits of English grammar: here, the poetic singer uses "one" as a collective pronoun. Neat trick. As a collective pronoun, it takes a plural verb, "the One / That interrupt...." It's grammatically impossible, but it works. A Robin is both One—and Many. More of this when we look at Keats's Nightingale. Pablo Neruda aims for a similar paradox in his opening poem to *The Art of Birds*. "Migration" tells how "All day, column after column, / a squadron of feathers ... nothing but orderly flight."

(Neruda, *Art* 15–16) Perceiving the many as one, Neruda sees

> Above the water, in the sky
> the innumerable bird flies on,
> the vessel is one,
> the transparent ship
> builds unity with so many wings ... (17)

Though I do not know many of the birds he writes of, his volume strikes me as the definitive austral bird literature.

Later in Dickinson's Robinsong poem she interprets what Robins say not by their speech but by their silence.

> The Robin is the One
> That speechless from her Nest
> Submit that Home—and Certainty
> And Sanctity, are best.

Dickinson interprets the Robin's values as what we call "home, motherhood and apple pie." Of course, the female Robin nests for only ten days, although she—and her mate—feed and teach offspring to forage for another couple of weeks. According to one source, the male Robin "cares for the fledged first brood while the female incubates the second batch." (Erlich 462)

Dickinson's earliest Robin poem, with which we began, is fine, despite its unfortunate line. About comparative standards, Dickinson is locative.

The Robin's my Criterion for Tune—
Because I grow—where Robins do—
But, were I Cuckoo born—
I'd swear by him—
The ode familiar—rules the Noon—
(Johnson, no. 285)

Later in the poem, she says "were I Britain born," she'd prefer nuts to daisies, disbelieve in snow, because even "The Queen, discerns like me— / Provincially...."

One who *was* "Britain born," John Keats, wrote the most famous bird poem in all Western literature, "Ode to a Nightingale." The title suggests the kinds of encounter that saint Giovanni di Bernadone and I have had in such differing ways, that is, an exchange between species. But Keats is no St. Francis, with his homiletic injunction to avian gratitude; still less is he like yours truly simply echoing and practicing bird language. Rather, Keats is a Romantic poet, and consequently he talks more to himself than to some birdbrain. He meditates on his heartache, his almost drugged numbness, his world-weariness which is punctuated and interrupted by the night song of the Nightingale. For me, a problem in translation arises here, because the closest American birdsong may be the Mockingbird's. (This raised a problem for Columbus, too, as we shall see.)

At any rate, the song or chatter of the Nightingale catapults Keats out of his local depression. He wants to become like the bird, first seizing on the quality of flight, "Away! away! for I will fly to thee." Realizing that such a wish to fly suggests either dreams or drunkenness, Keats denies it, "Not charioted by Bacchus and his pards," the most literary denial of inebriation in all literature. Picture, for instance, an officer stopping Keats and testing him for drink; Keats protests, "Officer, I am not charioted by Bacchus...." In his next line he immediately adds he will fly "on the viewless wings of poetry," but then drops this rather grand claim. In fact, he discovers somewhere in midpoem the real quality of the bird he admires and emulates—its song. That is what he wants to become, the singer, the immortal singer:

> Thou wast not born for death, immortal Bird!
>     No hungry generations tread thee down;
> The voice I hear this passing night was heard
>     In ancient days by emperor and clown:
> Perhaps the selfsame song that found a path
>     Through the sad heart of Ruth, when, sick for home
>         She stood in tears amid the alien corn....
>
> (Ferguson 511)

"No hungry generations tread thee down": does this mean, quite simply, that Nightingales are not game birds, nor are they much subject to predation? I don't know the history of hunting well enough, but this seems to be Keats's point. Perhaps even more, the song cannot be eliminated—except, as we know too well, and as did not occur to Keats, by extinction.

In the Nightingale ode, Keats knows immediately he envies the bird. He thinks at first he envies its capacity for flight. He tries flight as a metaphor, only to abandon it midpoem when he realizes that the claim that he is flying sounds drunken. This reminds us of how young this writer is. Keats drops his desire to fly for his real desire, that of any poet-singer, that his songs continue. Like the Nightingale's. Curiously, the bird's immortality is couched in its anonymity, its indistinguishability from other Nightingales. The One and the Many. "The voice I hear this passing night was heard / In ancient days...." Dickinson put it, "The Robin is the One." We can say that both Keats and Dickinson are specists. They can't tell one Nightingale, one Robin, from another. But this artful anonymity—to use Keats's phrase, this "Negative Capability"—assures the continuance of the song long after the singer departs.

Of course, Keats was somewhat wrong on "the voice I hear this passing night," which I can guarantee was not identical to any other heard on that night or "in ancient days by emperor and clown." As I have averred repeatedly, with scientific and experiential substantiation, each bird of each oscine species can be distinguished by its song; but usually the distinctions elude nonpasserines like us. Still, Keats's overall point is well taken, that song immortality requires a kind of anonymity. Neapolitan songs like *"O sole mio"* are sung today regardless of who specifically wrote and recorded them. And the poetry of any given language depends finally on the fortunes of that language, the ethnolinguistic "species" for however many centuries it may endure. For the student of Latin and Hebrew and Hindi, of Catullus and Solomon, "The voice I hear this passing night was heard / In ancient days."

Christopher Columbus the Genovan in Spanish employ made a classic mistake identifying a Nightingale. Leonardo Olschki has pointed out how Columbus functions by bringing what he knows—especially, his language for familiar objects—to what he does not know. We all do this. In this case, Columbus records in his *Diario* hearing an *ussignolo* on Hispaniola (Olschki). Of course, there are no Nightingales in the New World. What did he hear? My guess is some variety of Mockingbird, especially since Ehrlich et al. tell us, "unmated males sing at night in spring." (468)

The Nightingale is the most literary of birds, like springtime, a literary idea. Calendar spring includes some horrible weather, a high incidence of suicide for males in March, and many disappointments, but the literary convention of spring incorporates none of these. Similarly, the Nightingale is a noisy chatterer, but its literary associations suggest plaintive and unexpected melodies. In fact, the American Wood Thrush delivers what the Nightingale only symbolizes. The Wood Thrush sings at dusk in tall trees, lingering, resonant sequences, variations on a pentatonic scale. If you play all the black keys on a piano, that's a pentatonic scale.

But piano cannot render the Thrush's melodic suspension. The notes seem to float on the dark shadows under the tall trees, like a flute.

Often it sings two three-note series, the first two notes a descending minor third (to the tonic), the second and third a rising diminished seventh, this last note lingering. That's the first three notes. The second three start from the same note or one note higher in the pentatonic scale, rises one tone, and falls either a sixth or a fifth. And Thrushes often shift the base tonality, say from the key of E-flat—what sounds so, to one trained in tonal music—they may resolve to an F. At least, so I hear their deeply intriguing song.

Before I move on to Shakespeare and Catullus's birds, I linger over Dickinson. Her Oriole, what Thoreau calls a "Golden Robin," has the startling quality of *pennis*-envy. (God'll get me for that, since Dickinson's poem is a masterwork, a toccata or virtuoso arpeggio. And after all, Keats's poem is about *pennis*-envy, too. The Latin for "wings" is pronounced the way we say its cognate "pen" plus "ees." The pun works better on paper.) But surely "envy" is not too strong a word for her second line, her comparison of the Oriole's plumage to human plumage, and her own by implication.

One of the ones that Midas touched
Who failed to touch us all
Was that confiding Prodigal
The reeling Oriole —

So drunk he disavows it
With bandinage divine —
So dazzling we mistake him
For an alighting Mine —
    (Dickinson, no. 1466)

This is such a fine, extravagant poem that it's hard not
to keep quoting, especially because the next stanza
describes the Oriole's song, "A Pleader — a Dissem-
bler — / An Epicure — A Thief — / Betimes an Oratorio — / An Ecstasy in Chief —." What I have been
analyzing as the complex music of the Oriole, Dickinson calls "an Oratorio" and "badinage divine." Who
could disagree?

I think her "reeling Oriole ... so drunk" comes
from their feeding habits around, say, locust tree blossoms. I'm not sure whether they feed on the blossoms
or on the bugs that feed on the blossoms. Trusty
Ehrlich et al. say "spiders, some buds in spring," but
they grant nectar-sipping to the Hooded Oriole. (624)
In short, Orioles do move around as they feed. Upside
down, sideways, and so on. Of course, many birds do
this — winter Nuthatches, famously — but perhaps the
Orioles' brilliant coloration makes their motion more
obvious.

Dickinson calls them "the Meteor of Birds, / Departing like a Pageant / Of Ballads and of Bards." My other Amherst informant, Theodore Baird, once wrote me that those other brilliant birds, flocking Evening Grosbeaks at his feeder seemed like businessmen, well-dressed, aggressive. So whether birds seem sober or drunk depends upon how they must feed, and whether they're migrating, or *Zugunruhe*.

Finally, Dickinson's spectacular close. Like a Neapolitan author imbued in Greek and Roman myths, calling one coastal town for Aeneas's steersman Palinurus, another for his trumpeter Misenus, Dickinson becomes playfully mythy. Here's her Oriole.

> I never thought that Jason sought
> For any golden Fleece
> But then I am a rural man
> With thoughts that make for Peace—
>
> But if there were a Jason,
> Tradition bear with me
> Behold his lost Aggrandizement
> Upon the Apple Tree—

Wow. Talk about a Pageant. Of course, the poet takes a metamythic, skeptical attitude that is reminiscent of seventeenth-century English poets like Herrick and Marvell, "Fauns and Fayries do the Meadows till / More by their presence than their skill." (McDonald 43) Before we leave Dickinson's delicious avian evocation—admittedly, more visual than aural—we should note the poet's gender-bending in "I am a rural man." Writing in the nineteenth century, Dickinson chose, like George Eliot, the male persona, the conventional first person. "Chose" may be the wrong verb since it was foisted on the writer who planned to publish. Dickinson rejects publication in one famous poem, "Publication is the Auction / Of the Mind of Man." (no. 709) But then, she uses the published author's male persona.

Before leaving this great poet and fine ornithologist, I must note her Hummingbird. It is couched like a riddle.

> A route of evanescence
> With a revolving Wheel—
> A Resonance of Emerald—
> A rush of Cochineal—

Cochineal is a bright-red dye, so this exactly describes the only eastern species of Hummingbird, the Ruby-Throated, where only the male has a red throat. Both sexes have the bright metallic green above, "A Resonance of Emerald."

> And every Blossom on the Bush
> Adjusts its tumbled Head—
> The mail from Tunis, probably,
> An easy Morning's Ride—
>             (Dickinson, no. 1463)

Every blossom of, say, the orange trumpet-vine, nods as the fan-jet Hummer goes by. It appears and leaves almost magically, it "evanesces." One witnesses amazing stationary hovering, and then speed, like a rocket from Tunis.

Dickinson reenacts for us the experience of her seeing birds, like her other Robin poem,

> A Bird came down the Walk—
> He did not know I saw—
> He bit an Angleworm in halves
> And ate the fellow, raw. (no. 328)

After this brutal, thoroughly natural, candid event ("He did not know ... "), the Robin shows his civil grace by drinking "a Dew" from a "convenient Grass" (punning on "glass") and hopping aside to let a Beetle — otherwise a candidate for consumption? — pass. Dickinson observes the Bird's "frightened Beads" of eyes, how it seemed "like one in Danger." A brilliant observer of avian behavior, this poet recognizes the menacing world birds populate.

Shakespeare, on the other hand, appears to cite lore about birds as much as his own immediate impressions. For instance, he knows about the fascinating phenomenon we in America call the "Cowbird host." Cowbirds lay their eggs in any nest, and the female experiences no ovarian shrinkage after laying, so they have been termed "passerine chickens." (Ehrlich 619)

One species of Warbler, Kirtland's, has gone nearly extinct because it can't distinguish Cowbird eggs from its own, and the cowbird young, being bigger and more demanding, get the "Cowbird's share" of its dutiful though ignorant foster parents' harvest. Cowbird young also occasionally bite the parental feeder by mistake, sometimes fatally. (Cuckoo nestlings have been photographed pushing the eggs of rightful offspring out of the nest.) Shakespeare mentions the Kirtland's Warbler phenomenon in *King Lear.* As Goneril complains about her father's "insolent retinue," and about the Fool's freedom of speech ("this your all-licensed fool"), the Fool sings snatches of a song about Cowbird hosts (or in Europe, Cuckoo hosts).

> The hedge-sparrow fed the cuckoo so long
> That it's had it head bit off by it young. (1.4.198)

No sentimentalist, Shakespeare does cite lore and convention. His Sonnet 29 features the Lark as an image of gratitude to the creator, with or without Franciscan instruction. On thinking of his friend, the speaker recovers from his blues, from his solitary depression ("I all alone beweep my outcast state"), from his feeling "in disgrace with ... men's eyes." His mood, his "state" changes, "like to the lark at break of day arising / From sullen earth, sings hymns at heaven's gate."

But it would be hard to find better bird writing in Shakespeare than on those architects and domestic builders, Purple Martins. Perhaps it is fitting that the owner of New Place, the second largest house in Stratford, with its fourteen fireplaces, would notice avian housing. Toward the beginning of *MacBeth,* King Duncan arrives at the MacBeths' castle. He comments on the beauty of the place, its "pleasant seat," the nimble and sweet air. Banquo observes—high in the rafters of the Globe Theater?—

> This guest of summer,
> The temple-haunting martlet, does approve
> By his loved mansionry that the heavens' breath
> Smells wooingly here. No jutty, frieze,
> Buttress, nor coign of vantage but this bird
> Hath made his pendant bed and procreant cradle;
> Where they most breed and haunt I have observed
> The air is delicate. (1.6.3–10)

I must confess I have never seen Purple Martins in "pendant beds," although I know the birds from childhood.

They competed with my grandfather's Barn Swallows. The Swallows nested under the barn roof; the Martins inhabited my grandfather's large, two-story birdhouse, on a ten-foot pole. So I never saw their hanging nests, but I have seen abandoned Oriole nests overhanging roadways in winter, as did Thoreau one December:

> As we passed under the elm beyond George Heywood's, I looked up and saw a fiery hangbird's nest

dangling over the road. What a reminiscence of summer, a fiery hangbird's nest dangling from an elm over the road when perhaps the thermometer is down to -20 (?), and the traveller goes beating his arms beneath it! It is hard to recall the strain of that bird then. (Allen 288)

Ah, the song. Thoreau brings us back to our theme.

As for Purple Martins, Shakespeare also mentions them in *The Merchant of Venice,* where Aragon cites the Martlet as an image of common judgement,

> Which pries not to th' interior but, like the martlet,
> Builds in the weather on the outward wall
> Even in the force and road of casualty. (2.9.26–29)

These hanging nests, marvels of avian architecture, suggest the parrots nesting in Chicago, Jackson Park, and even an alley off Fifty-fourth Street, in Saul Bellow's recent *Ravelstein,*

> Like over-stretched nylon stockings, those nesting tenements where eggs were hatched drooped as much as thirty feet. (170)

Suspension nests, like suspension bridges, are marvels. Writers from Shakespeare to Thoreau to Bellow remark them in evocative language. English, too.

Other literatures evoke famous birds. The Romans had Catullus's well-known poem to his girlfriend's Sparrow, *Passer deliciae meae puellae.* (Cornish 2) It's about a pet, not a wild bird. For the Romans, birds were either food or pets. Or *en masse,* natural signs to be interpreted by a member of the college of auspices (like Cicero), if not an haruspex. Maybe those guys were better on bird flight than on entrails. Often they'd open up some beast and not find its heart. A very bad sign, they thought—though they didn't realize it was a bad sign for their training—the past, not the future. In Catullus's poem, he wishes he had a pet to relieve his loneliness, although he implies envy of the pet's intimacy. A précieux poet in seventeenth century France would have stated what Catullus implies, his wish to take the liberties a pet takes, nibbling index fingertip *(cui primum digitum dare appetenti),* pecking or lovebites, lying in her lap.

Return to the Robin we began with, but now the smaller English Robin much celebrated in poetry. The seventeenth-century preacher and wit Robert Herrick wrote "Upon Mrs. Eliz: Wheeler, under the name of Amarillis." In this twelve line epigram a "Robin-Redbrest ... brought leaves and mosse to cover her" until "Eliz" opened her eyes—which in the old science allows light to come out: "The lid began to let out day." (Herrick 49) A century later, William Cowper delights in this bird in midwinter,

> The redbreast warbles still but is content
> With slender notes and more than half suppressed:
> Pleased with his solitude, and flitting light,

From spray to spray, where'er he rests he shakes
From many a twig the pendent drops of ice ...

(Lack 32)

Again, probably the most famous English Robin reference occurs in Keats, this time in his "Ode to Autumn." In answer to the question, "Where are the songs of spring? Ay, where are they?" Keats writes some of the most lovely aural lines in English verse:

Then in a wailful choir the small gnats mourn
Among the river sallows, borne aloft
Or sinking as the light wind lives or dies;
And full-grown lambs loud bleat from hilly bourn;
Hedge crickets sing; and now with treble soft
The redbreast whistles from a garden croft;
And gathering swallows twitter in the skies.

(Ferguson 514)

What a closing! With the previous sounds of the cider-press oozings, the late bees, and now the lambs, the crickets, Robins and Swallows, Keats challenges the great literary dominance of spring. Spring is, after all, a literary idea, not the "real" spring of mud and flood, chill and roof leaks. In this ode, Keats chalks up one for Team Autumn.

Finally, Herrick's predecessor Edmund Spenser includes the English Robin ("Ruddock") in his exotic catalog of summer birds.

The merry Larke hir matins sings aloft,
The Thrush replyes, the Mavis descant playes,
The Ouzell shrills, the Ruddock warbles soft,
So goodly all agree with sweet consent,
To this dayes merriment. (Lack 32)

A fine example of Elizabethan plenitude in writing, Spenser repeats himself since both the Mavis and the Ouzell are Thrushes, as is, arguably, the Ruddock. But who demurs with taxonomical correctness?

The English Robin, much smaller than the American, certainly compares in aggressiveness. In *The Descent of Man and Selection in Relation to Sex* (1871), Charles Darwin—who may be called a literary author in that he calls Nature a "she"—remarks on the bird's fatal aggression in captivity. (Baird)

Mr Weir was also obliged to turn out a robin, as it fiercely attacked all the birds in his aviary with any red in their plumage, but no other kinds; it actually killed a red-breasted crossbill, and nearly killed a goldfinch. (Lack 165)

Even in the wild the English Robin displays similar behavior, as David Lack writes after quoting Darwin.

That intruders are recognized is evident enough, since in nature the owning robin promptly drives from its territory all other robins which try to enter, the bird's own mate only excepted. On the other hand, birds of other kinds are not usually attacked.... (Lack 165)

I seem to have crept into my next chapter, on foreign birds, already. That's the nature of literature; it takes one beyond one's own experience.

Before moving on, probably the second-most-famous bird in English literature, after Keats's Nightingale, is the "dapple dawn-drawn Falcon" of the nineteenth century English Catholic priest Gerard Manley Hopkins. (Recall that Robert Herrick, too, was a priest, an Anglican.) Of course, Hopkins' capitalized "Falcon" is not our mere species name, it is a Christological image, certified by the title, "The Windhover, To Christ Our Lord."

> I caught this morning morning's minion, kingdom
> of daylight's dauphin,
> dapple-dawn-drawn Falcon, in his riding
> Of the rolling level underneath him steady
> air, and striding
> High there, how he rung upon the rein of a
> wimpling wing
> In his ecstasy!
> (Ferguson 662)

Hopkins apostrophizes "the achieve of, the mastery of the thing!"—the thing being virtuosity of flight, which the poet takes as an image of religious ecstasy, and perhaps of Christ's rising from death. This grand poem should be quoted in its entirety, but it describes bird *flight,* not song. The Falcon doesn't speak. If He did, I suppose it would be heresy. And, of course, you could argue it's not about a bird at all.

Similarly, Andrew Marvell's justly famous "The Garden" includes these birdy lines comparing the soul to a bird.

> Casting the Bodies vest aside,
> My Soul into the boughs does glide:
> There, like a Bird, it sits and sings,
> Then whets and combs its silvery wings;
> And, till prepared for longer flight
> Waves in its plumes the various light.
>
> (Ferguson 275)

Marvell's lines seem even less about a bird than Hopkins'. Both poets are religious or philosophical and theological. Marvell's birdlike soul apparently derives from Plato and the Neoplatonics. In his next stanza, Marvell launches into a witty argument about prelapsarian man in his "happy garden-state / While man there walked without a mate." He ends this stanza with the puzzling ironic paradox, "Two paradises 'twere in one / To live in paradise alone." I am tempted to call this anti-Romantic, but Marvell seems to recommend

solitude, whereby he anticipates the Romantic poets—
and of course prepares the way for the Romantics'
rediscovery of his poetry.

Asian cultures offer marvelous birds in art and
poetry, my single example coming from China, Li Bo's
"Waking from Drunkeness on a Spring Day," where
the poet feels life is a dream—with Spanish playwright
Lope de Vega and many Shakespeare characters. In Li
Bo's case, the speaker uses it for an excuse to drink:

> Lying helpless at the porch in front of my door
> When I woke up, I blinked at the garden-lawn;
> A lonely bird was singing amid the flowers.
> I asked myself, had the day been wet or fine?
> The Spring wind was telling the mango-bird.
> Moved by its song I soon began to sigh,
> And as wine was there I filled my own cup.
> Wildly singing I waited for the moon to rise;
> When my song was over, all my senses had gone.

Here is an epigrammatic version of Keats's Nightingale. Keats longs for a "draught of vintage"; in the
English way, his pleasure is deferred, giving rise to the
great literature of the isle. Had Keats drunk more, he
may have written less, like Li Bo. The metaphor of
birdsong-poets' song is identical, although Keats first
wants to be like the bird in flight. Drunk, it's a good
thing Li Bo doesn't explore that bird quality.

In short, poets have always observed and described birds and found in them an image of exaltation or skyey message. Catullus's Sparrow-pet, Spenser's Ruddock, Shakespeare's Lark and Martlet, Herrick's Robin, Keats's Nightingale and gathering Swallows, Dickinson's Oriole, Robin and Hummingbird, and Hopkins' Falcon all form a vast catalog. We may call it an aviary, attended and nursed by the literary imagination.

_Titmouse_

# North Atlantic Birds

*B*IRD IS A UNIVERSAL LANGUAGE, a lingua franca, like Esperanto. At the risk of sounding like an ad in the *Times* travel guide, after a few days' practice you really can talk to natives in any country— France, Italy, Brazil, Japan, China. Of course, you'll be talking to native birds. You're unlikely even in suspicious nations to be breaking any local spy ordinances.

To start close to home, offshore: One midnight watch crewing on a sail from Jacksonville to Massachusetts, I heard our mast ringing. Some lashing or fitting made a *ping* on the alloy. Behind me over our wake something was echoing that ring. It was following us along in the moonlight, a fairly small bird, I think a Petrel, probably Wilson's. This was in late May. Was it enamored of our boat's mast? Talk about impossible relationships. During the day we saw them all the time, Mother Cary's Chickens. Wonderful fliers, they breed in the Antarctic, as do some Terns.

A couple of years ago I was enough lucky to spend a month on the south coast of England, in Dorset. The month of May, no less. Mixed with the sounds of lambs bleating and occasional cows mooing, now and again a shotgun popped in the near distance across the vale toward the pre-Roman earthen forts, Coney's and Lambert's Castles. Damp and overcast most mornings, there was always a cheering bird singing his dotted eighths, repeatedly. A Blackbird. English Blackbirds really do sing melodies, not just the inimitable *scree* and *wree* of our marshland variety. Hence Paul McCartney's song, "Blackbird singing in the dead of night / Take your broken wings and learn to fly / All your life / You were only waiting for / This moment to arise." That Blackbird's song was imitable, though varied. Here are my notes—well, really his notes, though at least one of his is a microtone, the second accented note, between A and G-sharp.

His song swings. In fact, I composed a jazz piece on the basis of this bird, as I did another based on the pentatonic, bluesy song of the American Wood Thrush.

I prefer the English Blackbird because I can imitate it, while the multivocal Redwinged Blackbird makes dozens, perhaps hundreds of inimitable vocalizations. Beletsky classifies the "alert" calls alone into: *peet, check, chuck, chick, chonk, chink,* and *cheer*. What I termed a *scree*, he calls the territorial call-note, a *conc-a-ree*. There turns out to be much scientific study of

Redwing song because of "the relative ease of conducting field studies on the species."(Beletsky 84) Redwing marshes are relatively confined spaces with high bird populations; hence the birds' social and vocal behavior can often be surmised. For instance, speakers broadcasting recorded Redwing song were aggressively perched on by male Redwings, and approached even by females.

Among those who have studied Redwing song are R. W. Simmers (1975), D. G. Smith and F. A. Reid (1979), K. Yasukawa *et al.* (1980), and Donald Kroodsma and F. C. James (1994). Les Beletsky summarizes their findings by raising issues that apply to all the bird species we mention: geographic variation, birds' learning new songs into their second year, and the effect of their gathering at large winter roosts on uniformity of call over their large range. (87)

Returning closer to home, what about the Loon? Here's a bird whose southernmost habitat lies in our northernmost states. Are Loons foreign? Not exactly. Sharing the lands of the Moose, they call amidst vast silences, at night. Their nocturnal call is at once lonely and very social, for of course another Loon responds. They call at other times, but not while feeding. I saw a pair in late afternoon on the headwaters of the Androscoggin, just after seeing a Great Blue Heron and, at another section, a young Moose eating salad. Some sort of water lily. The Loons dove at will; when I called, the male stretched his neck to see, but was not

fooled. The pair did converge, though. They continued to preen and raise one wing so they looked white-
backed, or rub their necks on their backs—neat trick.
They have oil glands in their mouths to "paint" their
feathers after diving. A few minutes earlier on this
August evening, with occasional trucks and vacation-
ers' vans going by, I heard a Loon across a half-mile
cove, beyond an island. I returned its call, and it called
back. In broad daylight. I have read that they give one
of their calls only when separated, a locative "Where are
you? I'm here."

In the second week of August, in Rangely, Maine,
after all the roaring car engines die down around 3
A.M., an occasional Loon calls. Again, theirs is a minor
third, flutelike, not a whistle. One of the slowest birdcalls, the notes are held, about one per second. Do they
wait for the cackle of humans to die down? The motor-
cycles and big pickups, the last motorboat with running lights on the lake. I don't hear their "laughing
Loon" call, hyena-like. Instead, they flute a quarter
note, hold it a second, rise a minor third, and slur it a
quarter tone down. The next time, it glissandos or slurs
a quarter tone up. Finally, they start the same, but then
end on the initial note.

So plaintive, or is it "plangent"? The Loon's call
goes right to my bones. It seems to tell me something of
vastness and timelessness, qualities that Keats taught
us to associate with birds. I walk to the side of the lake
and hear a couple of splashes under the half-moon.

Looking up at the moon through birders' binoculars I can see Crater Riccioli, named for himself by the man who named all the visible lunar features in 1651, Giovanni Riccioli. Does our Loon call to the *lunar?* If so, Moon-day, Monday (in French, *lundi*) may also be the Loon-day. Most other birds, owls excepted, call to the sun.

In the land of the sun, near Naples, one summer I heard birds chattering in tall conifer trees. This was at the Villa Vergilliana above the amphitheater at Cuma, one of the oldest in Italy, just now being excavated. Earlier I had heard from the masonry inset windows what I took to be Italian Blackbirds, tuneful, like the English ones. Something about all the masonry in Italian towns lends an echoic quality to sounds at a distance—Italian mamas calling their sons' names, for instance in the Santa Lucia district of Naples. Or birdsong through masonry inset windows. What I'm calling Italian Blackbirds sound burbling and bluesy, not pure-noted. They are syncopated so:

Blackbirds are not the only birds common to suburban Italy. Count on roosters at dawn.

Back in the New World, up along the St. Lawrence riverway, one morning I trod a *Sentier Ornithologique,* a Birders' Path. An insistent, repetitious bird called from the conifers bordering the riverbank. It was a rising call, just one tone. A Goldfinch, I think. There are many up there. I've seen a half-dozen feeding in a gravel drive two or three miles from the river. After all, it was thistle time, and the Goldfinch so prefer thistle seed that the French call them "Thistler," *Chardonneret*. The Goldfinch speech I'm most familiar with is an insistent in-flight call, falling just one tone.

One French name for a bird species can be read by those of us who do not have French. It's the onomatopoetic moniker Wood Peewee, spelled in French, Pioui. Say it like Peter Sellers' In-spec-teur Clusot. *Pi*, pronounced "pee," and *oui*, the French for "yes," pronounced "wee." To French ears, does this bird sound like a yes-man? Perhaps. The English name sounds like micturition—pee-pee and wee-wee—but I doubt any native English speaker associates the bird with urination. I have conversed with Peewees on South Mountain in the Berkshires. Even in mid-August, like a Titmouse in spring, a Peewee can be "called" by echoing his song. However, they stay in higher trees, verdure virtually the same as Wood Thrush habitat. From his considerable height the Peewee makes his onomastic sound, a fairly piercing rising glissando. Starting around the E an octave above middle C, the Peewee slurs up just shy of an F-sharp. To my ear, it's not exactly a full tone, although I could be wrong. The more I concentrate on birdsong, the more subtle and unrepresented by human notation it seems—even the modern notation in Gardner Read's books. Lots of variable birdsong quarter tones, for instance.

There surely is a cross-cultural as well as a cross-species aspect to birdsong. Onomatopoeia reveals a culture. Take the American sound for a cat, *meow*, and the British *mew*. Which cat sounds better bred? Which would your prefer in your house? Which would you prefer to stalk the attic for those pesky mice that scratch all night? Or consider the Russian verb for a dog's bark, *lyalyat'*. That's a puzzle for English speakers until you see a Russian film in which Borzois appear. In fact, Borzois on a hunt make exactly that sound, a kind of gulpy, almost gull-like bark—*Lya-ee, lya-ee*. Despite the hunt culture they share with the Russians, the English words evoke domesticated dogs, "woof" or "bow-wow." While I have heard dogs make a suppressed *wuhf*, I have never heard them bow-wow. In Italy, dogs *abbaiare*. Although clearly an imitation of dogs, onomatopoetic, it derives from Latin and Greek. According to Battisti and Alessio, the Italian Maritime Alp speech preserved the Latin baubare from the Greek *bayzo*.

Horses whinny. For American speakers, they do. To the English they *neigh*, to the Russians, they *rjat'*, to the French, *hennir*. But when I heard a carriage-horse in Quebec one hot August day, that horse pierced me with the equine condition. A handsome fellow, though no longer young, he was pulling a carriage with an overweight tourist not so different from myself, and an overweight driver. His mouth around the bit showed a bit of white foam. His whinny lasted maybe six seconds, *Whi-hih-hih-hnih-hny*. It was a *cri de couer* from a stout-hearted beast. I thought immediately of Jonathan Swift's marvelous representation of horse language in Book Four of *Gulliver's Travels*. The race of horse-philosophers call themselves, as might eighteenth-century human philosophers like Leibnitz, *the perfection of nature,* or Houyhnhnm. Their species name is a whinny. They despise the humanoform Yahoos, from which word derives their name for disease, *hnea-yahoo*. Anything bad is named using the suffix *yahoo,* as an ill-constructed house, *ynholmhnmrohlnw yahoo*.

Like Gulliver, I have spent more time learning from animals, very little time in educating birds, though I did try to teach one Oriole the famous theme from Beethoven's Fifth Symphony. According to the accounts, St. Francis did "preach" to birds, enjoined them to gratitude—which one would have thought they already expressed in many ways. At least, Gerard Manley Hopkins suggests the Windhover flight expresses his ecstasy. Mostly, then, we learn from them. No-one has learned more from birdsong than the French composer Olivier Messiaen. He researched birdsong like a field scientist, rising well before dawn in the spring, going to specific spots to hear specific birds. Wood Thrushes—*la grive des bois*. Blackbirds—*le merle noir*. Bluebirds—*le merle bleu*. Owls—*la chouette hulotte*. Larks—*l'alouette lulu, l'alouette calandrelle.* Buzzards—*la buse variable.* And again and again, Robins—*le rouge gorge.* Half of his six pieces in *Petites esquisses d'oiseaux* (1985) are titled *Le rouge-gorge.* He captures what I cannot imitate. Messiaen's compositions come the closest to that broad spectrum of inimitable birdsong that I have heard from Blackbirds and even Orioles, once you return their call-note "dial tones." It's no surprise that Olivier Messiaen's only opera, a massive work, is titled *Saint François d'Assise.* This French composer preceded me in the topic of my book, but his excurses are in music.

Messiaen and his wife made many field recordings of birds all over the world. In two compositions from the fifties, he develops his field notes:

> Actually, in *Oiseaux exotiques* [1955–56], I've linked percussion with woodwinds, brass, xylophone, glockenspiel, and piano, and this percussion obviously plays no part in bird songs; it constitutes a strophic support based on rhythms, verses, and Greek metric feet, and also on Hindu rhythms, all juxtaposed—the strophic form ... evolves independently of the bird songs, whose freedom is much greater. So there's a blend of strictness and freedom, and, all the same, a certain element of composition in the "bird-song material," since I've randomly placed side by side the birds of China, India, Malaysia, and North and south America, which is to say, birds that never encountered each other.
>
> (Messiaen, 1994, 131)

An earlier composition keeps to birdsong, and interestingly, chronobiology, from the predawn awakening into the night.

> In *Réviel des oiseaux* [1953], the presentation is much more accurate: there's really nothing but bird songs in it, without any added rhythm or counterpoint, and the birds singing are really found together in nature; it's a completely truthful work. It's about the awakening of birds at the beginning of a spring morning; the cycle goes from midnight to noon: night songs, an awakening at four in the morning, a big tutti of birds cut short by the sunrise, forenoon songs, and the great silence of noon. (Messaien, 1994, 131)

Note that Messiaen's exhaustive study of birds led him to adopt their sense of time. Their voluble day really begins predawn, and it seems to end for Messiaen at "the great silence of noon." In a performance by the Boston Symphony Orchestra (2 March 2002), avian microtones were achieved by dissonant notes on, say, violin and piccolo or the highest octave on the piano in combination with the ethereal celeste. Messiaen builds to the chaotic "big tutti of birds," which does sound like bird chatter at dawn—the mayhem of a spring sunrise. There is a delightful chaos of chirps and percussive rhythms—especially the five-beat rhythm discussed elsewhere. Then a Grand Pause, utter silence. The piece ends, after the piano's eighty-third to eighty-eighth keys work tirelessly for minutes. It ends with a wood block's simple tick-tock.

Three years after his exotic birds, the composer linked time and color to birdsong in *Chronochromie* (1959–60). One part of it, the "epode," scandalized his audience. Messiaen explains to Claude Samuel,

> It's written for eighteen solo strings—twelve violins, four violas, and two cellos—and it's made up of eighteen bird songs, all birds from France that sing together and who are, in order of entry, our blackbirds; a yellowhammer; the first goldfinch; a chiffchaff; a second goldfinch; a whitethroat; two chaffinches; a nightingale; a fifth and sixth blackbird; a greenfinch; two golden orioles, one of which echoes the other; and, a little later, a linnet and two garden warblers.
>
> These birds enter one after another, in something of a fugue, the entries proceeding on a descending scale; then all the voices go forward imperturbably, one on top of the other, achieving a counterpoint of eighteen parts totally independent of each other for at least ten minutes. (Messiaen, 1994, 132)

To Claude Samuels' question whether such a thing were possible in nature, Messiaen assures him that especially at daybreak one can hear "extremely complex counterpoints" produced by very different species united only by habitat. This scandalous part of *Chronochromie* gives rise, a quarter-century later, to the "Sermon to the Birds" in his opera *Saint François*. Of course, Messiaen's birdtalk is bispecial.

Just as I cannot imitate most Redwing songs without Messiaen's help (and a full orchestra), humans more generally can imitate only a small proportion of birdsong. Despite this, our songs often invoke those other, feathered vocalists—and not just French classical composers. Our best popular singers and musicians earn nicknames from birds, like the tenor saxophonist Charlie Parker ("Bird"), for whom the famous New York jazz club was named Birdland. Or the intense, beloved Parisian singer Edith Piaf, the "little sparrow." The popular songs they play and sing are filled with comparisons and references to birds.

Consider jazz standards such as "Skylark," "Robin's Nest" and Parker's own "Ornithology," century-old songs like "Mockingbird Hill," more recent songs like "When the Swallows Come Back to Capistrano" and rock songs like Paul McCartney's "Blackbird." The American songbook includes many bird references, like the verse from Johnny Mercer's "Too Marvelous for Words,"

> You're just too marvelous
> Too marvelous for words
> Like glorious, glamorous,
> … And so I'm borrowing
> A love song from the birds
> To tell you that you're marvelous,
> Too marvelous for words.

If that one is dictated by the "words-birds" rhyme, it is still a convincing use of it. One does not see it coming from a mile off, as with so many song rhymes: "blue-you," "you-true," "start-heart," and so on.

Occasional popular songs, like the Neapolitan *"'Nu Pasariello Sperzo,"* tell stories of birds — in that case, a displaced Sparrow chased, by lovers, even from the forest it takes refuge in. (Paliotti 92) Many other popular songs refer to singing, such as the laundry-girls' singing in the second verse of the famous *"O sole mio."*

There's no bird in this song, but the laundry-girl sings in the midst of nature after a storm.

> *'O sole mio*
> *Sta 'nfronte a te!*
> *Luceno 'e llastre d' 'a fenesta toia;*
> *'Na lavannara canta e se ne vanta*
> *E pe' tramante torce, spanne e canta,*
> *Luceno 'e llastre d' 'a fenesta toia.*
> *(Paliotti 126)*

Because this is Neapolitan, I shall not give a word-for-word translation, but metaphrase instead: "O my sun, keep before us. The glass in your windows is bright with sun, a washerwoman sings and vaunts, meanwhile wringing, clothes-pinning, singing." Our selection begins with the refrain which follows the first verse. Here I *do* translate word-for-word. "What a beautiful thing it is to see the sun in the serene air after a storm, why it's like a party already started." *(Che bella cosa è 'na jurnata 'e sole, / 'N'aria serena dopo 'na tempesta! / Per l'aria fresca pare gia 'na festa.)*

Jazz songs often conflate birds and women through the colloquial usage of "bird," as in Tadd Dameron's Lady Bird. In British usage, such a reference is entomological, a ladybug. I think not even rock music descends to the vulgar and obscene usage of "bird," as in the common gesture of "flipping someone the bird." All bets are off when it comes to rap music—though if biologists are right about the braggadocio of territorial birdtalk, birds are rappers, full of aggression. For the biologists, birdtalk is largely like gang insignia, the marking of territories.

*White-throated Sparrow*

# Winter Birds

NOT ALL BIRDS ARE TACITURN in winter, but don't expect their March chatter. Sometime in late October or November, the migratory species clam up. Even the resident Blue Jays and Titmice and White-throated Sparrows do not respond as the temperature hits freezing, or as their peers are flocking to migrate. This makes sense, after all. Besides weather and especially solar discussions, much birdtalk concerns property rights, their call-notes like avian Gold Rush prospecting claims. Surely only a bad-mannered Blue Jay would bring up his spacial needs in the midst of the crowd, the flocking delegates. So it follows that I should have expected precious little response when I called the firm, descending major third that only two days earlier had elicited a Jay flyby over my head. However, today was different. For one thing, there were ten or twelve Blue Jays within two or three small, thirty-foot trees. For another, they perhaps were exhibiting *Zugunruhe*.

While we may expect reticence, we also receive compensating gifts. Winter birds desperate for food appear at feeders close enough to touch. For birdtalkers, such an encounter is even more thrilling. We meet the little Sparrow with the white throat that we first heard in the deep pine woods of Maine. This January morning it's right here—in fact, a couple of them—on my front porch, its white throat patch outlined by a darker band. I feel as if I'm meeting a famous musician, a Wynton Marsalis or a Nina Simone. At the same time, I am meeting a correspondent, a pen pal, someone whose language—and moods—I've been learning.

I find this meeting of the remote creature a principle pleasure of the species engagement I attempt. How do a pet and a wild bird differ? Engaging a wild bird, birdtalking, is momentary and always terminable by the other party. Birdtalk is transient, though one may wile hours in such engagements.

Birdspace—roughly, for passerines, the ratio of thirty feet to one human yard—of course varies with species. Perhaps for an Eagle it's more like three hundred yards to one human yard. The point is, birdspace and birdtalk fit. Bird voices and bird patterns of life correspond, as do, I suppose, our American transience, mobility, and cell phones.

The snowlight gives a male Cardinal at the feeder a garish glow equal to his glissando song; I have seen wedding photographers on the Bay of Naples use large metal reflectors that give an effect similar to the snow. There are other surprises. The Titmouse has no cockade, probably concentrating too much on his or her food. I didn't know it retracted. This feisty little bird, so quick to defend its trees, here seems tame indeed. It's a bit sad, but we can intuit the meaning of "a state of nature." Winter must be got through, must be survived. For the humbled Titmouse, this snowday is not as exhilarating as any day in March.

But some birds do sing in near-freezing low-angle January sunlight. Although there are no flowers out in Kensington Gardens, London, nearby in a fenced, side-street green with access only to certain residents, Blackbirds start with high hawklike in-sucking calls. Like an Osprey, but firmer, harder. One flies from a huge plane tree behind some fourth-floor construction staging and plastic tarps. After I return the call, the bird sings a descending fifth plus a longer fourth:

Another Blackbird, I think, makes the staccato take-off series very like an American Robin. As I continue to mimic, one starts virtuoso, short trills and intervals.

Before toast (and dawn) the next morning, around 6, I hear a Blackbird in the green behind my room, the one that borders the parish church of St. Stephen's South Kensington. That's the church where T. S. Eliot headed the fire brigade in World War II. Its song is unaffected by the chill:

Later, walking Victoria Road to catch Bus #10, I hear a descending minor third with emphasis or accent on the second note, *dih-dah*. Along here the trees are smaller, decorating the small but elegant yards of the two-or three-story row houses. Only twenty feet away, I see the bird making the call; it's Chickadee-sized or a bit larger, in the top of a leafless tree. A black streak down its chest and belly separates the dusty yellow breast flanks. It's the same bird I heard a week ago over in Via Dezza, Milan. The Italians call it Cincerella, the Brits, the Great Tit. (Be careful about discussing this species in bars.)

Back home, in February, a high wind sweeps across the harbor bridge in my town. Invigorated, but with binoculars fogged, I have trouble identifying one of only two birds near channel rocks. Nearby a Black-backed Gull looks similar, except this one has a black chapeau on bright-white head and neck. I suspect the wings are black, though they're half-submerged. Peterson says the Black-crowned Night Heron "winters n. to s. New England (a few)." (16)

One cold morning in February I hear repeated Carolina Wren songs greeting the sunrise. The lengthening daylight trumps the temperature in bird values. And, as I have mused, the Carolina Wren may well feel that under the added cold the sun requires its special matins assistance in order to rise.

The last week in February, with the temperature about to rise to 50 degrees—but could the birds know *that?*—I see what looks like a small Robin, red-breasted, in a low leafless bush. Not on the ground. I get out my binoculars and notice a blue cap: It's the first Bluebird I've seen in three years. I go inside and look up Schuyler Mathews' version of its song, and also Cheney's. When I come back out, it's gone. I try the song by the book. No luck. Perhaps it is the song I heard walking home an hour ago in the village. One unfamiliar to my ear, plaintive, almost a trill. I thought it to be some Warbler. Maybe it was, but maybe it was this visitor.

Down by the salt marsh I hear Canada Geese in their usual racket of takeoff. Why do they talk so much during flight? Today, flapping and barking away they rise maybe two feet above the grass and hold that flightplan for a hundred yards until they're above water again. They keep yapping and honking another couple of hundred yards until they reach grassland; then they veer up over the near trees, still talking, and shortly fall silent. I presume they landed in a field just the other side of the junipers lining the far side of the river.

The mystery is—why all the noise? Contrast swans, notoriously mute even when not onomastically so.

Geese are more gregarious, more voluble. They seem to put more effort into flying, too. Perhaps they bark encouragements, rather like the "Go-go-go-go-go!" along the ski or decathalon routes at Olympic venues. Contrast the silence of the Hawks I see perched along the highway as I drive north at dusk through a dusting of snow. Every couple of minutes I notice another one ready to feed on a hapless rabbit crossing the road; or is he desperate enough to fend off the Crows from their roadkill? Only once at dusk was I surprised to see a Hawk feeding on roadkill, but it may have been an Owl. It was dark enough.

Living on the Eastern coastal flyway, and just within the holly range (read, fairly mild winters), I witness daily Canada Goose commuting. Sometimes I think our house is at the intersection of two gooseways. Truly, they are *highways,* a couple of hundred feet higher than where I stand. Gooseways never have cloverleafs. They don't even have proper 90-degree intersections, nor stop signs. They do include "yield" instructions, by word-of-beak. Geese wedges, sometimes two hundred strong, always cross in X's. They seem to know toward exactly which point on the compass they're heading. Unwavering, undeterred by the traffic at the intersection, they flap full-on. Yapping away, beating crosswind, two geese masses head onward. From the vantage of this flightless observer, they seem to be at the same altitude. But this cannot be true. Also, their voices, their *honks,* seem similar, but this again must not be so. I still must develop my ear to tell familial distinctions that allow such masses of traffic to converge, and then to proceed undeterred. In my experience only the French motorists at the *Place de la Concorde* operate with such straight-ahead minds. The place is a traffic circle, but the Parisians cut secants through it, like the gooseways over my yard.

_Song Sparrow_

# Spring Birds

*A*H YES, SPRING AND BIRDS—a tautology. When *is* spring? Birds define it with their return to northern climes. Swallows to Capistrano. Robins to the Emily Dickinson homestead. So "spring birds" is redundant. With the sighting of the first Robin, spring manifests itself, although recently there have been non-migratory Robins in southeastern New England. This year let us say spring begins with the first Bluebird, on February 20. The branches are bare, but filling with dozens of bird varieties. The air rings with minor thirds in a dozen timbres: Cardinals glissing up, Titmice glissing down, Chickadees with their two sustained notes stretching almost to a minor third, rare and tentative Bluebirds, and Robins still mostly silent while coursing the yard for worms, insistent Carolina Wrens, Mockingbirds, Warblers, and high Starlings in the range of Warblers.

I feel dazed, like a symphony conductor who has lost control. I doubt that I've even identified all the various singers, much less responded to them. I do respond to a Titmouse, who then varies his call. He first makes isolated calls with perhaps a quarter note rest between, but once I answer, he speeds up the series. When I repeat the faster version for a couple of minutes, he varies the rhythm into a rising call. The slight change sounds to me like a huge difference, from "Stay out of my tree," to "Come to my tree—so we can 'take it outside.'"

I remain about fifty feet away, under the bare branches of another tree, perhaps just outside the tree-line territory he is claiming. A couple of days later, I hear dueling Titmice, descending unslurred minor thirds, a half tone apart, as in the first two measures above. I do not enter the fray to confuse the issue.

At any rate, today is gray, nearly 50 degrees, and the myriad birdcalls fill the air with a Gold Rush, homesteading land-rush feeling. So many of these oscine passerines share similar notes in the octave above middle C; I reflect on the pond birds—Mallards, Black Ducks and Wood Ducks. It's the Mallards who almost sound like frogs today. Nuthatches, too, have a frog-like, cawing note, like a small Crow. They almost share language across species—an Amphibian-passerine summit.

When I arrive at work rushed, having parked far away, I hear a clear piped descending major third. Unmistakable. A Blue Jay, out of his myriad disguises. In a month this call will lose its second note and become, for a couple of weeks, just one piped, clarion call. For years it would surprise me every spring, so un-Jaylike. Yet it is the thing itself, the "Jaynote." A couple of weeks later, in mid-March, I make this jaycall to flocking Blue Jays. They fly closer, look at me. They don't return the call. It may well be a breach of etiquette, like saying "Bon voyage" to someone who has no upcoming vacation, or "Good morning!" at dusk.

One week into March, the predawn has a chaotic, festive and battleground feeling. Titmice echo, half a tone apart, from a hundred yards away. A trifle. Normal conversational range. When is the last time you talked to someone a hundred yards away? I'll bet you were on a boat. Or in a parking lot. It's remarkable, really. These little creatures, the weight of my little finger, assert themselves across—indeed, *occupy*—acres. With them are a Cardinal not yet warmed up and a Song Sparrow calling from far away, down by the open fields.

March 9 this year I talked to two song sparrows on my college campus. They were in two pathetic leafless trees planted last year; but they were near the water, and the song (only one sang) rebounded from the brick walls. They did not discuss their migration, although I asked. (I asked by trying variants on their song, hoping one would be Southern dialect.) What had they seen? Long Island? The Carolinas? They spoke of now, of the day, of their expectations. As if drunk with the sun, they spoke of their fond hopes, as if wars, crimes, and human evil did not exist.

A day later, another Song Sparrow dueled from thirty yards away. I couldn't see him, but I know the song. The initial rhythm is the same as the prior—"prior" only because of its location, closer to where one was sighted earlier. I couldn't swear they are the same song, or the same banded bird. A rough approximation of the duel goes like this:

The second ends with an in-sucking sound, here shown with discord. Both are quite different from the Song Sparrow between fields near my house fifteen miles away. No two Song Sparrows sing at all alike except for the initial rhythm.

Meanwhile the Cardinals are back. At first I confuse their initial shortened whiplike glissandos, rising minor thirds, with those of the Titmice, usually a bit lower. The Titmice's rising, slurred minor third is their "invitational" rather than their "confrontational" (descending, more staccato) call-note. They sound similar to an untrained ear, but I believe they have entirely different meanings. I have never heard the rising, invitational one used in a close-up battle for territory, whereas I have heard the descending, unslurred one used many, many times, often by two Titmice on contiguous branches.

The Cardinals, like the Jays, use their spectacular coloring to attract attention; the Cardinal song can attract plenty of attention, too. For the same effect, the Mockingbirds must jump and hover over topmost branches to display their white wingstripes. In early spring the Cardinals leap in song intervals, fourths and fifths, even octaves. Here I heard one slow down his song later (after the double bar).

On the Ides of March I see one perched halfway up a tree, not on top, making a descending triad, repeating it a couple of times, and then adding the usual whip-like glissandos. Shortly afterward, he flies down low (altitude three feet) toward my house and into shrubbery. Perhaps a nesting site. They have nested nearby in previous years. Pyrocanthus, you know, provides plenty of thorny protection.

Such a variety of similar songs among the Cardinals; as I leave my ATM one day I hear an unusual one, perhaps immature, or perhaps a Cardinal ideolect.

Instead of the usual triplet, there's a catch or a pause or a thirty-second-note rest between the first two slurred notes and the third (a harmonic "fifth"):

I go back into my small bank and tell the teller; she says she'll listen for it when she leaves in seven hours. With such ease we have all adapted to the human-made environment. Yet, look at what we lose—what *she* loses—in our disconnection from the natural or the wild.

## Gray Day

ONE RAINY MORNING a week later I talk to a Robin outside the small, shingled takeout bakery in town. Misty, the rain has paused right now. Lots of English Sparrows *cheep, cheep* in the nearest scraggy tree. I hear a few Robin plosives, which I wait to imitate because they are bird warnings—the kind of call they make when they spy a cat. Then, as in the prolog to this book, I purse my lips, but instead of in-sucking a *cheep* (also an avian warning), I burst one staccato, plosive note, tongued as if I played a bugle, flute, or trumpet. Ten seconds later I make another. Not sure of the effect of my returned warning, I see the Robin perhaps thirty feet away, making a couple of more plosives, then flying in back and above the little bakery. Now maybe fifty feet away, above the bakery, it starts a song. But instead of the usual burbling plenitude of alternating triplets and higher glissandos, descending, I hear a minimalist song—two glissandos, a fifth leap between:

I am amazed, almost astounded. Never have I heard such a reduced Robin song. Is it the gray, rainy weather? Feeding Robins often sing more strongly in rain. Could it be a female? In the poor lighting I don't really notice. What I do observe is warnings, lots of them. Over the course of the whole rainy day (later listening to the birds a half-hour away in Providence) is the full panoply of "Watch it!," "Careful, there!," and *Attenzione!* All in Bird, like so: *chk chk, cheep, chp, tssk, sskp,* and then the Robin's warning note I made earlier. Robins repeat that *sforzando* plosive in their flight song on takeoff, each note rising a half-step (or less, a quarter tone) in a series—often of five.

(See the rising chromatic call of the London Blackbirds, above in the last chapter, "Winter Birds.") Today I hear this call quite often, and all the assorted warnings of many bird species.

Are birds more threatened, more vulnerable to predators, in dark, gray weather? It appears so, on our evidence of one day late in March. Probably their enemies—feline, avian, and herpetological—all count on more success with reduced visibility. There are, of course, proverbial shades of gray. Today, the day after, is quite bright, though still overcast. I hear fewer warning notes, fewer raucous Robin flight songs. Perhaps, too, they can't use their own bright male colorings so easily to distract when all colors are reduced. And what do we know of bird vision in the gray range?

A week after that minimalist Robin, on another gray day, I hear two other birds using the same intervals. It may be coincidental, or it may be that short glissandos a fifth apart are the right calls for this leafless, gray April the second. At 5 A.M., predawn with only the dark outlines of buds and branches, I hear a Cardinal twenty-five feet from my roof-window. It's cold, maybe 35 degrees. Because he's close, I subdue my response, just the first two notes. To my weak notes (see after the double bar), he truncates his song as if listening. Probably he is. He reduces his song to triplets.

Ten minutes later, a Robin makes a burbling version of these same notes (the first two measures), with a few more sliding brief glissandos. Finally, I hear the same notes, now an octave lower, slower, and with such a different timbre or tone quality.

This is the Mourning Dove, like Cardinal or Titmouse recorded at 78 rpm and played at 33. I don't know what to make of these shared vocal gestures, shared tonalities, even. But surely they hear each other's similar phrases and know they use common notes. Of course, each bird's note—say F, an octave above middle C—made by Robin or Titmouse or Cardinal or Mourning Dove is distinct and recognizable, usually.

Spring birds, like flocking birds, use silence, as well. The silence of nesting birds, and especially nest-building birds, is profound. This same dark, gray April 2nd I opened my storm door to return a Robin's short "reports." It's dark, near freezing. I don't have my coat on. After fifteen seconds with no response, just before I close the door, something dark rushes from near the porch, almost under my feet. It's a Robin, perhaps the mate of or even the very bird I was talking to. It had fallen silent, searching perhaps for a nesting site. The song may have been simply to attract—and to distract—other creatures, as it had me.

A couple of minutes later I saw first one silent Robin, then another, dark apparitions in a nearby apple tree. Neither was singing, or had sung for awhile. Their business, their mission, required "radio silence." Often in nesting season a male Robin or Cardinal will sit on a top branch and give a spectacular display:

Meanwhile, the female flies low, entering or leaving the nest or nest-to-be. Having completed his distracting display, the male too flies low as the female did previously.

In the midst of their song, birds are their birdiest. Completely full of themselves and their music, thinking only of—rivals of the same species? They direct their song at other birds. They enact "speech acts," gestures that hold meaning for others of their species, and possibly other bird species. At their birdiest, songbirds remind us of ourselves. Most all human endeavor centers on other humans. And how limiting such a perspective is. Would Napoleon have invaded Russia because of something the Sturgeons did? Or the Yaks? Has any human ever declared war on the pets of another society? Although the consequences of war inevitably devastated the enemy's domestic animals, usually they were not "targeted." Let us be thankful that our species-blindness has at least this one minor blessing.

Early April in a cold snap, the wind is up. Where do they go, the birds? Closer to the ground, doubtless.

In the low 40s today; last night I observed a dozen gangly Great Egrets, big as Blue Herons, heading toward the pond. They pulled up just shy of it, in the tops of trees. Quite a sight, like Jason's golden fleece, but these were large white "fleeces" perched in medium-sized trees a hundred yards across a small pond. At 5 o'clock this morning they were still there, but gone by sunrise.

Walking by a larger pond this morning after very brief snowflakes, temperature in the low 40s Fahrenheit, I see a snaky, dark neck and upslanting, long bill. Cormorant, its body entirely submarine, as it often is. Then it "rows" (as Dickinson put it) in the air, paddling with its feet to get airborne as I do in my dreams. Fifty yards farther out a small ducklike critter pops to the surface. Using my binoculars I determine it's a Puffin just before it somersaults back into its feeding medium. None of these birds are talkative, though the passerines still repeat their calls in the cold. An exuberant Cardinal celebrates the dawn, along with a chorus of Titmice, Chickadees, and Song Sparrows.

I'm amazed next day in the wintery 40s, by how much energy the Titmouse shows with his constant rising major-third glisses and occasional more rapid descending minor thirds, often a half-step higher. He "covers" my yard and a neighbor's eight-acre field. When he's on the far side of it, I start my rising-third response. Although I can't see him over the knoll, with every response he sounds closer. And then he appears.

I vary my response so he won't think I'm challenging him. I decide to try a little Mendelssohn on him, the *Italian Symphony*. *Da-deed-da da-deed-da* (his major-third call) to which I add the fifth.

He responds with his same two rising glissandos. I do it again. His same again. But on the fifth or sixth try, after his two glisses and my Mendelssohn sound bite, I hear just the rising gliss from the third to the fifth. He did it! A joyful moment. He also flew back farther in the field. A mini-good-bye. Though he did not comprehend the whole phrase of Mendelssohn, he did understand an additional tone. We shared a musical idea.

Simple mimicry is not conversation, though it may act that way among birds parodying each other. Conversation requires saying something other than what is said to oneself. To converse with a bird, one must vary what the bird says. Recently, this spring, I began varying my imitations by a half-tone, or with shorter glissandos. I think that the less public, more domestic birdtalk—say, between mates—employs shorter glisses, as well as quieter.

I end this section on spring with my homemade poem on spring and its transition to summer. I give it a French title after a character in Shakespeare's *The Tempest*.

*Lai d'Iris*
Let the mouse-ear hawkweed dare
To challenge daisies, and appear
When the leaves their yellow trim
Sprinkle on the trunk and stem
Of wild cherry, flowering pear
And crabby apple. Let the year
Begin in strife, pugnacities
Of Wren and Warbler burst in spurts
Of bird barks. Let Robins fill
The gorse with nests, and Cardinal
Choose white-blossomed pyrocanthus,
Whose orange berries in the fall
Splash surprises where they will.
With the summer's midday yawn
Let the lilacs turn to lawn
And iris, second-yeared, grand-dam
Of the *fleur-de-lis*. Then butterfly-
Weed open like a symphony,
Bright with bees and those that name it,
Moth-sized, buying golden pollen
With their labor, dusted their wings
With it—or is it just the way
Themselves are dappled? And by now
The ox-eyed daisies follow purple
Loosestrife, joe-pye weed and dock,
Berries manifold, black or wine-
Berries, raspberries gone by,
But blue (wild ones) on mountainsides
In Richmond next to Tanglewood.
Now August's spiky thistle, sting-

Ing horse nettles, and rods on rods
Of goldenrod—the steeple kind, or
Cantilevered, the Thai dancer type—
Nodding, waving. These I've seen
Without a name; now they come
When I call them to this poem.

_Cardinal_

# Animal Language:
# The Linguistic Debate

O BIRDS, OR ANY ANIMALS, have an actual language? I have proceeded on the tacit assumption that for our purposes they do. I do this first to contradict the usual human-centered view. Second, it is a central assumption for interacting with birds as we have. But at this point it should prove useful to look at the historical discussion of language in both mankind and animals. In Noam Chomsky's *Cartesian Linguistics* we learn that seventeenth-century French thinkers such as Descartes, Cordemoy, La Mettrie, and Bougeant set the terms of this debate. In the next century the grounds of the debate shifted to German theories of the origin of language by Romantics like Herder and Schlegel.

Père G. H. Bougeant's *Amusement philosophique sur la langage des bêtes* (1739) suggests the tenor or register of the discussion. Bougeant states several ideas that recur until this day, for example, "tout le langage des Bêtes" reduces to expression of their sentiments and passions. Nor are those passions numerous. Following Locke, Bougeant argues that animals have no "abstract and metaphysical ideas." (Chomsky 11) In a passage that seems to describe Hartshorne's "non-versatile" songbirds, his monotonously repetitive class of birds, Bougeant says,

> *Il est nécessaire qu'elles répètent toujours la même expression, et que cette répétition dure aussi longtemps que l'objet les occupé.*

> It is necessary that they keep repeating the same expressions, and that such repetition last as long as the object occupies their mind.

Not only do they repeat the same expression in the presence of a specific stimulus, but they cease to repeat it when the object no longer strikes their senses: *"Elles n'ont que des connoissances directes absolument bornées a l'objet présent et matériel qui frappe leurs sens."* (Chomsky 11) Many modern ornithologists, such as Alexander Skutch, also attribute birdsong to immediate sense data and their resulting affects.

Birdsong at dawn, under Bougeant's theory, results from the sighting of auroral glimmer. Skutch agrees, but adds that song results from heightened emotions. I have speculated that there may well be an abstract or "metaphysical" addition to these, that birds act as if their song helps the sun to rise. The more they join in and participate, the more albal success they have. Most do not sing anywhere near as much—as often or as long—on overcast days. On a windy, cold March day there is virtually no birdsong, while yesterday, in the

6os, they were legion. Toward dawn, it's as if they begin cheering, praising the sun, and as it gratifies their praise and cheer, they sing more.

John Locke raises the issue of bird language a half-century before Bougeant in *An Essay Concerning Human Understanding*. Under his discussion of simple ideas, and particularly their retention, Locke says:

> This faculty of laying up and retaining the *ideas* that are brought into the mind, several *other animals* seem to have to a great degree, as well as man. For, to pass by other instances, birds learning of tunes, and the endeavors one may observe in them to hit the notes right, put it past doubt with me that they have perception and retain *ideas* in their memories and use them for patterns. For it seems to me impossible that they should endeavor to conform their voices to notes (as it is plain they do) of which they had no *ideas*. For though I should grant sound may mechanically cause certain motion of the animal spirits in the brains of those birds whilst the tune is actually playing; and that motion may be continued on to the muscles of the wings and so the bird mechanically be driven away by certain noises, because this may tend to the bird's preservation: yet that can never be supposed a reason why it should cause mechanically, either whilst the tune was playing, much less after it has ceased, such a motion in the organs of the bird's voice as should conform it to the notes of a foreign sound, which imitation can be of no use to the bird's preservation. (1.122)

Locke appears to refer to some account of bird learning, perhaps the same by the "most learned Dutchman" referred to in Thomas Fuller's preface to *Ornitho-logie; or, the Speech of Birds*. Fuller says that the Dutchman "hath maintained that Birds doe speake and converse one with another: nor doth it follow, that they cannot speake, because we cannot heare, or that they want language, because we want understanding."(A2)

More likely Locke refers to some native English experiments with birdsong, for he concludes specifically in regard to bird imitation of nonbird sounds, sounds that were in fact produced on the previous day. This seems very like the kind of naturalist intervention reported at the new Royal Society.

> But which is more, it cannot with any appearance of reason be supposed (much less proved) that birds, without sense and memory, can approach their notes nearer and nearer by degrees to a tune played yesterday; which, if they have no *idea* of in their memory, is now nowhere, nor can be a pattern for them to imitate, or which any repeated essays can bring them closer to: since there is no reason why the sound of a pipe should leave traces in their brains which not at first but by their after endeavours should produce the like sounds; and why the sounds they make themselves should not make traces which they should follow, as well as those of a pipe, is impossible to conceive. (Locke 1.122)

I can't claim in all my interactions with birds that one ever reiterated a tune produced yesterday better the next day. The closest I came was in "teaching" Beethoven to an Oriole. He rejected the final cadence, nor did he improve the next day. Having said this, I must admit the avian training Locke intimates suggests Tchernichovski's experiments with mechanically programmed plastic birds. (See chapter 5, p. 79.)

Locke's most famous passage on birds concerns a parrot in Brazil. Like most discussions of animal language, this one focuses on the bird's learning human speech, rather than our learning his—as we endeavor to do. Soon after his discussion of metempsychosis, Locke regales his reader with the story of Prince Maurice.

> I had a mind to know from his own mouth the account of a common but much credited story, that I had heard so often from many others, of an old *parrot* he had in *Brazil* during his government there, that spoke and asked and answered common questions like a reasonable creature, so that those of his train there generally concluded it to be witchery or possession; and one of his chaplains, who lived long afterward in *Holland,* would never from that time endure a parrot but said they all had the devil in them. (Locke 1.279)

Locke assesses what one might call the courtroom demeanor of the witness, "[Prince Maurice] said, with his usual plainness and dryness in talk...," that there was some truth to it, that he had asked upon his arrival in Brazil the parrot be sent for, though a great way off. The bird turned out to be very large and old:

> When it came first into the room where the Prince was, with a great many *Dutchmen* about him, it said presently: *What a company of white men are here?* They asked it what he thought that man was, pointing at the Prince. It answered, *some general or other.* When they brought it close to him, he asked it: *D'ou venez-vous?* It answered De Marinnan. The Prince: *À qui êtes-vous?* The parrot: À un portugais. Prince: *Que fais-tu là?* Parrot: *Je garde les poules.* The Prince laughed and said: *Vous gardez les poules?* The parrot answered, *Oui, moi, & je sais bien faire,* and made the chuck four or five times that people use to make to chickens when they call them.

Quite a little conversation, about what strangers always ask: What do you do? I watch the chickens, *cluck, cluck.*

Now, this whole conversation was originally in "Brazilian"—not clear whether Locke means Portuguese, or dialect, or a native language. One would assume that since the parrot belongs to a Portuguese man, he would have taught it Portuguese. Locke continues:

> I set down the words of this worthy dialog in *French,* just as Prince Maurice said them to me. I asked him in what language the *parrot* spoke and he said in

*Brazilian.* I asked whether he understood *Brazilian;*
he said no, but he had taken care to have two inter-
preters by him, the one a *Dutchman* that spoke
*Brazilian,* the other a *Brazilian* that spoke *Dutch;*
that he asked them separately and privately, and
both of them agreed in telling him just the same
thing that the *parrot* said. (Locke 1.280)

Locke concludes that the "Prince at least believed himself in all he told me, having ever passed for a very hon-
est and pious man." He leaves it to naturalists to reason,
and to others to believe as they please. For our purposes, the parrot's ability to mimic human speech, even
on a "baby Greek" level, is less to the purpose than its
owner's ability to communicate with the bird. Did it
ever confide where its enemies roosted?

The mid-seventeenth century saw the growth of
inquiry in natural philosophy—what we now call "science"—such as aberrations at birth, or "monstrosity."
With this study of what we now call "genetic defects"
came discussions of what defines "man." Locke cites
the example of a French abbot, Mon. Ménage, whose
defects at birth stymied the priests. They wondered if he
should even be baptized:

Nature had moulded him so untowardly that he was
called all his life Abbot Malatrou [i.e., ill-shaped]
.... This child was very near being excluded out of
the species of man, barely by his shape ... but no
reason why a rational soul could not have been

lodged in him; why a visage somewhat longer, or a
nose flatter ... could not have consisted with such
a soul. (Locke 2.56)

What bodies may a soul inhabit? This impinges on
our subject if language is a principal evidence of mind
or soul. (For the Greeks they were both *psyche*.) The
idea of animal languages then, like pet cemeteries, treads
the edge of heresy, as it also stretches the limits of com-
passion. For instance, it turns out that the complex
social life of ants includes a language, partly stridula-
tion, a certain squeaking. And ants can hear caterpillars,
in their own interspecific encounters. (Milius 93) But
the language of insects defies human sympathy. Nor
do the ancient Pythagoreans or Hindus, as far as I
know, include ants in their hierarchy of souls.

Birds, on the other hand, keep appearing as symbols of the soul in the Western tradition, and apparently in some non-Western traditions—Native
American and Asian. An example from English Literature arises late in Andrew Marvell's famous poem
"The Garden." (See chapter 7.) Paradoxically, to claim
that birds have souls is heresy in orthodox Christianity.
At the same time, birds are common symbols of the
soul in that same tradition.

*Chickadees*

# Birds of America

ROCK MUSIC FANS TOOLING ALONG in open-windowed Camaros, motorcyclists on BMWs and Harleys, women mowing lawns, motorboaters, suburban men on riding lawnmowers, moped commuters, golf-course greenskeepers with weedwackers, joggers with earphones plugged into cassettes or CD players, joggers even without earphones (too exhausted to listen), residents near airport landing strips, people who live along the flight paths of smaller corporate and private planes, riparian residents when the hydroplane is running, the same bankside residents when motorboats grace the river, coastal dwellers during high surf, everybody on a stormy night, most everybody on a stormy day, cyclists with earphones and CD players, long-haul truckers in big rigs, cyclists whose own thumping hearts drown out everything, local delivery van drivers, all motorists with car windows closed, most motorists with them open, trash collection drivers and workers, those with ear damage from rock concerts, those with ear damage for any other reason, and ... the deaf. These are some of the people who can't hear the birds. They can't hear them, or they don't listen, or they can't be bothered. For many of them, birds are trivial, their songs negligible compared to a rock song.

Even if they wanted to hear the birds, and say, the peepers, the frogs, the crickets, the squirrels, and so on, it's getting harder to do. In an interview broadcast on national news, Bernie Krause, who records natural sounds professionally, estimated that when he started out he needed ten hours to come up with a one-hour recording without motors, jets, and other human sounds. Now it's more like two-hundred hours to one. His interest is biophony, the natural panoply of sounds across the wavelengths that enable the various natural necessities — frogs camouflaging themselves in cacophony that distracts predators, scarce birds finding mates. (Krause 3; Beebe 5) Our mechanical and human sounds seriously impair this basic order, or disorder.

For those who could not care less about birdsong, they themselves — and since the list once included me, *we* — have much in common with birds. We Americans are constantly on the wing, moving long distances in a single day. To work — an average commute of twenty minutes to half an hour — and home again. To the store. Large proportions of our Northeast residents migrate south for the winter, to Florida or the Southwest. They have even acquired the appropriate name of "snow-birds."

When we see flocks of starlings moving *en masse* from power line to rooftop and back, or two flocks of Canada Geese crossing in some imagined interstate interchange in the sky, or even Sandpipers scurrying on the beach at the water's verge, don't we see our own behavior, too? What are our daily commutes but short flights. And for the last fifty years we have been flying all over—literally. Air traffic is nearing gridlock. Where is everyone going? Where we are not. What are we looking for? Food and nesting sites—and a lot that birds don't need. Better plumage. Better interest rates for retirement accounts. Airline tickets.

Still, the fundamental comparison of bird behavior and human behavior, especially with regard to movement, is probably more true now than at any time in human history. And most true in the United States. Most of us are involved in massive movements on a daily, seasonal and yearly basis. The hectic life of the suburban SUV mom, picking up this child from school, dropping at lesson one (say, tennis) or at organization two (say, Boy Scouts), driving on to child number two's school, and so on: what is this but fledgling tending, following the brood through the undergrowth, often done by male bird parents, while the female nests the second batch. For most of the birds I mention, fledgling tending lasts no more than a couple of weeks, though at that stage the young will continue to flock with their parents for migration. And in certain cases, year-old young will return next season—that is, after the long haul south and then north again—with its parents. A few springs ago I saw a Bluebird group of three, apparently mates and offspring, check out my Bluebird house. They did not stay. It was only a one-bedroom, studio birdhouse.

I wonder if that third Bluebird, which I take to be last year's offspring, is male. In Italy this would be the *mammone,* the mama's boy who refuses to leave the nest, even into middle age. In the States, the male off-spring still in home residence through his twenties is more likely to be a rock musician. Several of my successful friends with large houses have such resident offspring, usually sons. They are the singer-sons, as I noted with songbird gender. They are the Bluebird young, the songbirds of our culture.

Of course, other flocking birds, such as Canada Geese, also migrate with their offspring. Comparisons can be made here, too. As Konrad Lorenz showed, most Geese species are monogamous. The Canada Goose, throughout the menaces and confusions over long distances of migration must well benefit from the close affiliation of such pairing. It may well benefit the flock as a whole; with such large flocking birds and a near-even balance in sex ratio, might not annual or seasonal turmoil over mates really disrupt a species' ability to survive?

Christmas letters from old friends make me think of nothing if not avian behavior. "Daughter Sammy's in the Northwest, but she'll be flying to join our son in Germany. We'll all meet up at Dusseldorf before...." How did we as a nation get so compulsively airborne? Everyone has a different story leading to the same cumulative result. For some, army service took the daughter or son overseas to Italy, to Germany. Others studied languages which they improved by one of the many international study programs now available. This in turn led to more extended stays. For some, exchange students initiated the fatal attraction of distant cultures. For others, it was family—and not just in one country. Often the father's family is from Italy, the mother's from Ireland. Finding one's "roots" can be a lifetime occupation. It involves lots of travel, of flying around. Whatever one's own roots, the root of "immigration" is "migration." The birds know about this.

We sapiens certainly dreamed of flight long before we could do it. Leonardo da Vinci's winged man is a recent example, "recent" in terms of the history of flight. Swinging from trees is not too different from flight, gravitationally. It's a beautiful, sinusoidal series of arcs. Probably the oldest part of our brain controls flight in the sense of "fleeing." What is your own personal border between flight distance and attack distance? When is someone "in your space"? Of course, it depends on whether we're at work or in our car or at home, on the sidewalk in a crowded city, on wide sidewalks in Denver or narrow Roman ones in Pompei. Stopping at an automatic toll booth to fling some quarters, I saw an attendant three feet away waiting to cross behind my car. I said "Hi." He didn't respond. Why would he? If he were in the booth he would have. But caught "in flight," he was not official greeter for the turnpike. He had no "flight song." Some birds—many birds—don't.

We're talking about Walkmans and car radios and walkie-talkies or cell phones with speakers always on— all the paraphernalia of human audio. Surely cell phones, like airplanes, bring us closer to bird behavior. Now, like birds, we can emit on a regular basis territorial calls. I'm here. Who's out there? Where are you? This is kind of interchange never was necessary prior to mobile phones. You know when you call a home phone or an office phone exactly where your interlocutor is. When calling someone at their house, you'd be crazy to ask, "You at home?" Or when you call someone at their office, "You at the office?" Not likely. If you've been to their house, you can picture the exact room, even what's on the wall, when you call someone's home phone. Same goes for an office phone, if you've been there. Of course, you rarely do picture such locations (unless you're in love). Location is not the principal content or signification for most phone calls prior to cell phones. Now, like the birds, we talk of *where*.

This morning, for instance. Gray and warm, early August. I hear a glissando, rising. It's a Cardinal, though this call is different from the Cardinal songs I heard yesterday. Whiplike, it glissandos up a fourth, and then *poom!* It accents the beginning note again. I repeat the same call. It repeats the whiplike glissando, but not the *poom*. What's going on? Possibilities: The glissando says, "I'm here, in my tree." The *poom* adds, "Alone." When I join in, it drops the "alone." That's possible, but not probable. Maybe my *poom* was unconvincing, or otherwise incorrect. Perhaps the *poom* signifies "at some distance," and when I answered, the distance was less, so the *poom* wrong. Perhaps the *poom* functions like a proper name in sapiens, "I am here in my tree, I the Cardinal Giuseppe." This is least likely of all; I am mixing several types of human signification, including individual identity, rare even in human cultures. Are any of these right? I don't know, but I do know the songs are very different on a gray morning in August from the songs on a sunny morning in May or June.

Why? Begin with chronobiology, the time element in biologic functions. Mating, for example, has strong chronobiological parameters. Most species mate in spring. Territorial selection usually relates to mating as well as feeding. Different songs exist for each. Then consider the anxieties of birdlife—where are the rest of its species? Will the sun rise? Will a Kestrel or other avian predator show up, swift and silent? Will a snake or Jay dine on its embryonic young in their shells? Birdsong may express these anxieties, though it doesn't seem to, except in their *keck-keck* warnings.

While most writers divide songs or vocalizations into spring and fall (or winter), in fact, these are better divided into "lengthening-day" and "shortening-day" songs. Recall the English Robin, whose "spring song" begins in late December, just after the shortest day at the winter solstice (December 22). Consider also all the new songs from the "same old" birds, the ones we hear in late July or early August, *chick-a-dee* being one. Previously, the Chickadee is a clear minor third. The distinctive minor thirds of Chickadee and Titmouse and Oriole differ in timbre or tone quality, like the difference between an oboe and an English horn, or a French horn and a fluegelhorn playing the same note. Or Ray Charles and Paul McCartney singing "Yesterday." Anyone can tell the difference, but you have to have heard them before.

Compared to many elaborate *in situ* recordings and scientific publications on bird vocalizations, my method—if it can be called that—must seem amateur indeed. Since the root of *amateur* is "lover," from Latin *amo, amare,* I readily accept that I am a lover of bird-song, an amateur. But I would argue that my approach to understanding birds, my attempt even to respond and communicate with them in some rudimentary way, may serve as a model for the grander destiny of our species. About the time Shakespeare began writing (and parenting his first child), Giordano Bruno claimed that all the stars in the night sky are really like our sun, that moreover they probably, like our sun, have planets around them, many of which are inhabited. For this idea, which he called the infinite number of habitable worlds, and for seven other, more common heretical ideas, he was burned alive in Rome's Campo dei Fiori. The day was February 17, 1600.

Fast-forward to our twenty-first century. Pick up the *New York Times,* scan the front page. Several times in the last few years a news piece has appeared on the discovery of stars whose motions suggested the presence of planets, some of them huge, many times the size of Jupiter. Giordano Bruno's heretical perception is still front-page news. No inductive evidence of intelligent life on other planets yet exists: nor did Bruno proceed as his successor Galileo did. But the existence of the millions or billions of galaxies, each with millions of stars, surely attests to Bruno's insight. And when we meet up with these creatures from other worlds, how will we proceed? We can use our Earthly encounter with other species as a model. Our first communications are bound to be on the order of call-notes or dial tones. They will be locative, as with cell phones. "We are here. Where are you?" They will also be call-notes in that they will claim Earth as ours and no one else's. Stay out of our tree.

# Works Cited

Allen, Francis H. *Thoreau on Birds: Notes on New England Birds from the Journals of Henry David Thoreau.* Reprint ed. Boston: Beacon Press, 1993.

Armstrong, Edward A. *A Study of Bird Song.* Reprint ed. New York: Dover, 1973.

Ayer, Alfred Jules. *Language, Truth and Logic.* New York: Dover, 1946.

Baird, Theodore. "Darwin and the Tangled Bank." *The American Scholar* 15 no. 4 (1946): 477–86.

———. "Corn Grows in the Night." In *Thoreau's Walden and Civil Disobedience.* Edited by Owen Thomas. Norton Critical Edition. New York: W. W. Norton, 1966.

Baptista, Luis F. "What the White-Crowned Sparrow's Song Can Teach Us About Human Language." *Chronicle of Higher Education* (7 July 2000), B8.

Battisti, Carlo, and Giovanni Alessio, *Dizionario Etimologico Italiano.* Firenze: G. Barbèra, 1950.

Bean, Michael, and Melanie Rowland. *The Evolution of National Wildlife Law.* 3rd ed. Westport, CT: Praeger, 1997.

Beebee, Trevor J.C. *The Natterjack Toad.* Oxford: Oxford University Press, 1983.

Beletsky, Les. *The Red-Winged Blackbird: Biology of a Strongly Polygynous Songbird*. London: Academic Press, 1996.

Bellow, Saul. *Ravelstein*. New York: Penguin Books, 2000.

Bonora, Maurizio. *Uccelli di campagna*. Verona: Edizioni l'Informatore Agrario, 1994.

*Bulletin of the Nuttall Ornithological Club*. 7 & 8. (1882).

Burtt, Harold. *The Psychology of Birds*. New York: MacMillan, 1967.

Burton, Frederick R. *American Primitive Music, with Special Attention to the Songs of the Ojibway*. Reprint ed. Port Washington, NY: Kennikat Press, 1969.

Burton, Robert. *Comment nourrir les oiseaux de l'Améerique du Nord*. Abridged ed. St. Laurent, Quebec: Éditions du Trécarré, 1997.

Caelius Aurelianus, "On Chronic Diseases [Methodici Siccensis tardarum Passionum]." In *On Acute Diseases and On Chronic Diseases*. Edited and translated by Israel Drabkin. Chicago: University of Chicago Press, 1950.

Caldwell, Mark. "Polly Wanna Ph.D.?" *Discover* 21 no. 1 (2000): 69.

Catchpole, C.K., and P. J. B. Slater. *Bird Song: Biological Themes and Variations*. Cambridge: Cambridge University Press, 1995.

Catesby, Mark, FRS. *The Natural History of Carolina, Florida and the Bahama Islands*. 2 vols. London, 1731.

Cheney, Simeon Pease. *Wood Notes Wild: Notations of Bird Music*. Boston: Lee and Shepard, 1892.

Chomsky, Noam. *Cartesian Linguistics.* New York: Harper and Row, 1966.

Cicero, M. Tullius. *De Senectute; De Amicitia; De Divinatione.* Translated by W. A. Falconer. Loeb Classical Library. Cambridge, MA: Harvard University Press, 1964.

Cornish, Francis Warre, ed. *Catullus, Tibullus and Pervigilium Veneris.* Loeb Classical Library. Cambridge, MA: Harvard University Press, 1966.

Danforth, Susan, Curator, and William McNeil. *Encountering the New World 1493–1800.* Providence, RI: John Carter Brown Library, 1991.

Deacon, Terrence W. *The Symbolic Species: The Co-Evolution of Language and the Brain.* New York: W. W. Norton, 1997.

De Saussure, Ferdinand. *Course in General Linguistics.* Edited by Bally and Sechehays. Translated by Wade Baskin. New York: Philosophical Library, 1959.

De Tovar, Juan. *Historia de la Benida de los Yndios.* Mexico, 1585.

Dickinson, Emily. *The Complete Poems of Emily Dickinson.* Edited by Thomas Johnson. Boston: Little, Brown, 1960.

*Dizionario Napoletano.* Amato and Pardo. Milan: Antonio Vallardi, 1997.

Ehrlich, Paul, David Dobkin, and Darryl Wheye. *The Birder's Handbook: A Field Guide to the Natural History of North American Birds.* New York: Simon and Schuster, 1988.

Elliott, Lang. *Know Your Bird Sounds.* 2 vols. NatureSound Studio, 1994.

Falls, J. Bruce, "Functions of Territorial Song in the White-Throated Sparrow." In *Bird Vocalizations,* edited by R. A. Hinde. Cambridge: Cambridge University Press, 1969.

Fenton, William N. "Northern Iroquoian Culture Patterns." In *Handbook of North American Indian.* Vol. 15, edited by Bruce Trigger. DC: Smithsonian, 1978.

Ferguson, Margaret, Mary Jo Salter, and Jon Stallworthy, editors. *The Norton Anthology of Poetry.* Shorter fourth edition. New York: W. W. Norton, 1997.

Flood, Renée Sansom. *The Lost Bird of Wounded Knee: Spirit of the Lakota.* New York: Scribner, 1995.

*Fontes Franciscani.* Edited by Enrico Menesto and Stefano Brufani. Assisi: Edizioni Porziuncola, S. Maria degli Angeli, 1995.

Fuller, Thomas. *Ornitho-logie, or, the Speech of Birds.* Lodon [sic]: Printed for John Stafford, 1655.

Guthrie, Ramon, and George Diller, eds. *French Literature and Thought Since the Revolution.* New York: Harcourt, Brace and World, 1942.

Habig, Marion, ed. *St. Francis of Assisi, Omnibus of Sources. Writings and Early Biographies.* Quincy, Illinois: Franciscan Press, 1991.

Harris, Roy. *Language, Saussure and Wittgenstein: How to Play Games with Words.* New York: Routledge, 1988.

Hartshorne, C. "The Monotony Threshold in Singing Birds." *Auk* 72: 176–92.

———. *Born to Sing: An Interpretation and World Survey of Bird Song.* Bloomington: Indiana University Press, 1973.

Hay, John, ed. *The Great House of Birds: Classic Writings About Birds.* San Francisco: Sierra Club Books, 1996.

Heizer, Robert, and Albert Elsasser, *The Natural World of the California Indians.* Berkeley: University of California Press, 1980.

Herman, Louis, and Sheila Abichandani. "Dolphins (Tursiops truncatus) comprehend the character of the human pointing gesture." *Journal of Comparative Psychology.* 113 (Dec. 1999): 347.

Herrick, Robert. *The Poems of Robert Herrick.* London: Oxford University Press, 1960.

Hinde, R.A., ed. *Bird Vocalizations.* Cambridge: Cambridge University Press, 1969.

Hirschfelder, Arlene, and Paulette Molin. *The Encyclopedia of Native American Religions.* New York: Facts on File, 1992.

Hoxie, Frederick E., ed. *Encyclopedia of North American Indians.* Boston: Houghton Mifflin, 1996.

Hudson, W. H. *Afoot in England.* London: J. M. Dent and Sons, N.D.

Hutson, H.P.W. *The Ornithologists' Guide, Especially for Overseas.* London: British Ornithologists' Union, 1956.

Keats, John. "Ode to a Nightingale." In *The Norton Anthology of Poetry.* Edited by Ferguson et al. Shorter fourth edition. New York: W.W. Norton, 1997.

Kightley, Chris, and Steve Madge. *Pocket Guide to the Birds of Britain and North-West Europe.* London: Pica Press, N.D.

Kircher, Athanasius. *Musurgia universalis, sive ars magna consoni et dissoni.* Rome: Haenedium Francisci Corbelletti, 1650.

Krause, Bernard L. *Into a Wild Sanctuary: A Life in Music and Natural Sound.* Berkeley, CA: Heyday Books, 1998.

Kristeva, Julia. *Language, The Unknown. An Initiation Into Linguistics.* Trans. Menke. New York: Columbia University Press, 1989.

Kroodsma, Donald E., and Edward H. Miller, eds. *Ecology and Evolution of Acoustic Communication in Birds.* Ithaca, NY: Cornell University Press, 1996.

Lack, David. *The Life of the Robin.* London: Witherby, 1965.

Lawall, Sarah and Maynard Mack, eds. *Norton Anthology of World Masterpieces,* vol. 2. 7th edition. New York: W.W. Norton, 1999.

Li Bo, "Waking from Drunkenness on a Spring Day." Translated by Arthur Waley. In *Gems of Classical Poetry in Various English Translations.* Edited by Lu Shu-xiang and Xu Yuan-zhong. Hong Kong: Joint Publishing Co., 1988.

Locke, John. *An Essay Concerning Human Understanding.* 2 vols. London: J. M. Dent, 1961.

Lorenz, Konrad. *King Solomon's Ring.* New York: Crowell, 1952.

MacKay, Barry Kent. *Bird Sounds: How and Why Birds Sing, Call, Chatter, and Screech.* Mechanicsburg, PA: Stackpole Books, 2001.

Margoliash, Daniel. "The Song Does Not Remain the Same." *Science* 291, no. 5513: 2559.

Marler, Peter, C. S. Evans, and M. D. Hauser. "Animal Signals: Motivational, Referential, or Both?" In *Nonverbal Vocal Communication: Comparative and Developmental Approaches.* Edited by Hanus Papousek, Uwe Jurgens, and Mechthild Papousek. Cambridge, UK: Cambridge University Press, 1992.

Mastro, Jim G. "Signal to Noise." *The Sciences* 39 no. 6: 32.

Mathews, F. Schuyler. *Field Book of Wild Birds and Their Music.* New York: The Knickerbocker Press, G. P. Putnam's Sons, 1910.

Messiaen, Olivier. *The Technique of My Musical Language.* Translated by John Satterfield. Paris: A Leduc, 1956–61.

Messiaen, Olivier and Claude Samuel. *Olivier Messiaen: Music and Color: Conversations with Claude Samuel.* Translated by E. Thomas Glasow. Portland, OR: Amadeus Press, 1994.

Metz, R. C. *Langenscheidt's Standard Italian Dictionary.* New York: Bantam Books, 1990.

Michelet, Jules. *L'Oiseau.* 2nd edition. Paris: Hachette, 1876.

Milius, Susan. "When Ants Squeak." *Science News* 157 no. 6: 92.

Miller, Olive Thorne. *Bird-Ways*. Boston and NY: Houghton Mifflin, 1885.

Morris, D. "A Semiotic Investigation of Messiaen's *'Abime des oiseaux,'*" *Analles Musique,* viii (1989): 125–58.

Neruda, Pablo. *Art of Birds [Arte de pajaros]*. Translated by Jack Schmitt. Austin: University of Texas Press, 1985.

———. *Canto General*. Trans. Jack Schmitt. Berkeley: University of California Press, 1991.

Nice, Margaret. *Studies in the Life History of the Song Sparrow*. 2 vols. New York: Dover, 1964.

Nottebohm, Fernando. "Brain Pathways for Vocal Learning in Birds: A Review of the First Ten Years." In *Progress in Psychobiology and Physiological Psychology* 9 (1981): 85–124.

Olschki, Leonardo. *Storia Letteraria delle Scoperte Geografiche*. Firenze: Olschki, 1937.

Paliotti, Vittorio. *Storia della canzone napoletana*. Rome: Newton Compton Editori, 1992.

Pasquier, Roger F. *Watching Birds: An Introduction to Ornithology*. Boston: Houghton Mifflin, 1977.

Pepperberg, Irene, and Sarah Wilcox. "Evidence for a Form of Mutual Exclusivity During Label Acquisition by [African] Grey Parrots (Psittacus erithacus)." *Journal of Comparative Psychology* 114 no. 3: 219.

Peterson, Roger Tory. *A Field Guide to the Birds, Eastern Land and Water Birds*. Boston: Houghton Mifflin, 1947.

———. *Le Guide des Oiseaux du Québec et de l'Est de L'Amérique du Nord*. Traduction de Blain, Cyr, Normand, et Gosselin. Boucherville, Québec: Broquet, 1999.

Peterson, Roger, Guy Mountfort, and P. A. D. Hollom. *Guida degli Uccelli d'Europa*. Translated by Massimo Pandolfi and Sergio Frugis. 3rd ed. Padova: Franco Muzzio, 1988.

Pinker, Steven. *The Language Instinct: How the Mind Creates Language*. New York: Harper Perennial, 2000.

Powers, Alan W. "Head over Googols." *New York Times Magazine,* 9 August 1987, 10. Reprinted International Herald Tribune.

Powers, William K. *Sacred Language: The Nature of Supernatural Discourse in Lakota*. Norman, OK: Oklahoma University Press, 1986.

———. "Songs of the Red Man." *Ethnomusicology* 14 no. 2: 358–69.

Read, Gardner. *20th-century Microtonal Notation*. Westport, CT: Greenwood Press, 1990.

Rossinsky, Natalie M. "'Going Ape' over Language," *Odyssey* 10 no. 7: 10.

Saunders, Aretas A. *A Guide to Bird Songs*. New York: D. Appleton-Century, 1935.

Saussure, Ferdinand De. *Course in General Linguistics*. ed. Bally and Sechehaye. Translated by Wade Baskin. New York: Philosophical Library, 1959.

Schleidt, W., et al. "Störung des Mutter-Kind Beziehung durch Verhöverlust," *Behavior* 16 (1960): 254–60.

Shepard, Paul. *Encounters with Nature*. Edited by Florence R. Shepard. Washington, DC: Island Press, 1999.

Simmers, R. W. "Variations in the Vocalizations of Male Red-winged Blackbirds (Agelaius phoenceus)." Ph.D. thesis, Cornell University, Ithaca, New York.

Shakespeare, William. *William Shakespeare: The Complete Works*. Compact Edition. Edited by Stanley Wells and Gary Taylor. Oxford: Oxford University Press, 1992.

Skutch, Alexander F. *The Minds of Birds*. College Station, TX: Texas A&M University Press, 1996.

Smith, Anne M., ed. *Shoshone Tales*. Salt Lake City: University of Utah Press, 1993.

Smith, D. G. and Reid, F. A. "Roles of the Song Repertoire in Red-winged Blackbirds." *Behavioral Ecology and Sociobiology* 5 (1979): 279–290.

Specter, Michael. "Rethinking the Brain: How the Songs of Canaries Upset a Fundamental Principle of Science." *The New Yorker* (23 July 2001): 42–53.

Sprague, J. M., and A. N. Epstein, eds. *Progress in the Psychobiology and Physiological Psychology* 9 (1980).

Sturtevant, William, general editor. *Handbook of North American Indians*. Washington, DC: Smithsonian Institution, 1976–88.

Swift, Jonathan. *Gulliver's Travels and Other Writings*. Ed. Miriam Starkman. New York: Bantam Books, 1967.

Taylor, Kip. *Loon*. Saranac Lake, NY: Kip Taylor, 1988.

Thielcke, Gerhard A. *Bird Sounds*. Translated by John Drury. Ann Arbor: University of Michigan Press, 1976.

Thorpe, W. H. *Bird-Song*. Cambridge UK: Cambridge University Press, 1961.

Waldbauer, Gilbert. *The Birder's Bug Book*. Cambridge: Harvard University Press, 1998.

Weed, Clarence, and Ned Dearborn. *Birds in Their Relation to Man*. Philadelphia and London: J.B. Lippincott, 1903.

Williams, Roger. *A Key into the Language of America*. 1643. Reprint edition. Ann Arbor: Gryphon Books, 1971.

Yasukawa, K. "Territory Establishment in Red-Winged Blackbirds: Importance of Aggressive Behavior," *Condor* 81: 258–64.

Young, Jon. *Advanced Bird Language*. Audiocassette. OWLink Media, 1999.

*Gull*

# Acknowledgments

In addition to those listed in my notes, I have received a wide variety of help. I am indebted to librarians at the British Library and at Brown University—particularly those at the Science Library and Susan Danforth at the John Carter Brown Library—as well as to Dr. Gabriela Adler at my own Bristol Community College Library. This book could not have been written without the inspiring conversation of Richard C. Wheeler. I am indebted to music instruction in computerized notation from Prof. Andrew McWain, to a crucial music loan from Judy Conrad, and to operatic discussions with Richard Clark. I have prospered under the philosophical tutelage of Dr. Bill Kaufmann. My conversation has improved from long association with the raconteurs Ben Guy and Michael Miller.

One could not have settled among more generous and expert neighbors than Rick and Marge McNally, Jennifer McIntire, Marie Hadfield, Harriet and Bill Barker, and Selena and Jim Howard. Birders such as Philip Sheehan and Kevin and Deborah Lawton have fostered my interests. The writers Jamie O'Neill and Tim Coutis have inspired me, as have the scientists Drs. Jon and Liz Wolpaw, and Dr. Dave Warr. My colleagues Art Lothrop, Joe Murphy, and John Majkut lighten our daily teaching load. Former students like Mark Bisson, Mark Folco, Omayra Fontanez, and Mark Sardinha leave me grateful. Finally, Isaac and Laura Segal, Rev. David M. Powers, Marie Ged and Dan Mallett, Dr. C. "Ben" Lindsay, and Dr. Jean D'Amato Thomas have been unwavering supporters.

It is customary to record last one's greatest debt, to the creature (not a bird in this case) who illustrated and illuminated this manuscript and my life.

# Index of Birds

# General Index

# Index

ALAN POWERS graduated from Amherst College in 1966 and earned his Ph.D. in English from the University of Minnesota in 1974. Since that year he has been on the faculty at Bristol Community College, where he was Chairman of the English Department from 1988–1992. A scholar of Renaissance Italian, English, and American literature, he has published and lectured widely on Shakespeare, Giordano Bruno, Seventeenth Century and Romantic poets and poetry; as well as Emily Dickinson and other American writers. Interested as much in local history as language, his interests include research and publishing on early American New England street games.

He has held many fellowships and prizes for research and his own poetry, and in 2001 made a guest appearance in James Wolpaw's documentary film on Emily Dickinson.

Powers lives in Westport, Massachusetts, with his wife, the artist Susan Mohl Powers.